# Madame Butterfly

# Madame Butterfly

Japonisme,

Puccini,

 the Search for

the Real

Cho-Cho-San

Jan van Rij

STONE BRIDGE PRESS
Berkeley, California

*Published by*
STONE BRIDGE PRESS
P. O. Box 8208, Berkeley, CA 94707
TEL 510-524-8732 • sbp@stonebridge.com • www.stonebridge.com

Credits appear with their respective images, except for: artwork on pages 34 and 152 by
Rossi and Myrbach from Pierre Loti, *Madame Chrysanthème* (Paris: Calmann-Lévy, 1888);
photograph on page 84 from Giuseppe Adami, ed., *Giacomo Puccini: Briefe des Meisters* (Lindau-
Bodensee: Werk-Verlag Frisch and Perneder, 1948); photograph on page 150 from Myoko
Kishimoto, ed., *Koe—Ochofujin—Miura Tamaki* (Tokyo: Fubunsha, 1947).

Jacket design by Stephanie Young.
Text design, map, and charts by L. J. C. Shimoda.

Printed in the United States of America.

10  9  8  7  6  5  4  3  2  I     2006 2005 2004 2003 2002 2001

LIBRARY OF CONGRESS CATALOGING-IN-PUBLICATION DATA
Rij, Jan van.
    Madame Butterfly: Japonisme, Puccini, and the search for the real Cho-
Cho-San / Jan van Rij.
        p. cm.
    Includes bibliographical references.
    ISBN I-880656-52-3
        I. Puccini, Giacomo, 1858–1924. Madama Butterfly.  I. Title.
ML410.P89 R55 2000
782.I–dc2I
                                                                00-046395

*to Kei*

# Contents

# *Preface*

OF ALL THE OPERAS, WHY DID I CHOOSE *MADAMA BUTTERFLY* FOR a historical analysis? I have loved operas ever since I saw my first one, Gounod's *Faust*, in 1944 in Amsterdam during the last gruesome winter of the war. The opera was performed by undernourished singers and with daylight cleverly directed by mirrors as the only illumination of the scene. This rare experience may have generated my predilection for opera as a genre. Puccini's typical brand of *verismo* and his "burning intensity of feeling" (as Mosco Carner called it) always seduced me. But my special interest in *Madama Butterfly* has been enhanced very much by my confrontation with the title character in her hometown of Nagasaki.

The first time I went to Nagasaki was in 1986 as part of a private trip I made with a friend to the southern island of Kyushu, to break away from the routine of Tokyo where I was posted at that time. We duly visited the local tourist attractions such as Pierre Loti's house and Glover Garden. Pierre Loti's original house in what is now called Juninmachi, where he lived with O-Kane-san (better known under her name in the novel, Madame Chrysanthème), has of course long since been replaced by another one—Japan's wooden houses have only a limited life. The garden, however, must be about the same as it was originally. The view of the bay is gone because of the dense construction around the area now. A big stone memorial in the street marks the fact that Loti lived there.

Glover Garden is an open-air museum housing foreign residences of the late Edo (1603–1867) and early Meiji (1868–1912) periods and covering a part of the area of the old foreign concession. It draws large numbers of Japanese tourists, mostly schoolchildren and honeymooners. Steady flows of visitors are swallowed up by an ugly escalator system that brings them to the top of a hill; from there they walk down through a number of alleys and stairs that pass by old residences and offices. About halfway down the hill is one of the major attractions: a small terrace with a beautiful view of the city and the bay, dedicated to Madame Butterfly and her tragic fate. In front of a stone wall with a waterfall, a small statue pays tribute to Miura Tamaki, the first Japanese soprano ever to perform the title role in Puccini's opera (an event that took place in London in 1914). The statue shows Cho-Cho-san with her son Trouble; she is pointing to the bay where one fine day Pinkerton might reappear. Hidden loudspeakers reproduce the aria "Un bel di vedremmo" ("One Fine Day") and the "Humming Chorus." A marble bust of Puccini looks down at the scene. Young Japanese newlyweds have their picture taken in front of the statue, in spite of the risky symbolism.

With the *Butterfly* drama thus injected into his or her mind, the visitor continues the descent and on the next plateau enters Glover Mansion, the oldest Western-style wooden house in Japan. It was built in 1863 by a Japanese carpenter for the Scottish merchant Thomas B. Glover. Photographs, life-size mannequins, and signboards give an overview of the public and private life of Glover and hail his contributions to economic and political changes in Japan in the latter part of the nineteenth century. They also convey the presence of a Mrs. Glover, a Japanese by the name of Tsuru, represented here in a black kimono with white butterflies embroidered on the sleeves, and of two children: a daughter, Hana, and a son, Tomisaburo. No further explanation is given; no other details are supplied. One leaves the house in a state of confusion: What is this? Glover Garden or Butterfly Garden? Japanese tragedy or foreign success? Where do the stories join?

There are official answers to these questions, kindly supplied by the municipality of Nagasaki, which responded to the need to set up an important tourist attraction. The local Association for the Preservation of Cultural Assets and the Nagasaki Chamber of Commerce decided that the most effective way of making this project successful was to relate it to Puccini's opera. In doing so, the municipality spokesperson explains, they were well aware that Butterfly is the heroine of a novel and an opera, not a real person, but they thought that their little trick would be effective and wouldn't harm anybody. After all, nowhere was it said that Mrs. Glover was the same person as Butterfly. The association simply created a little ambience and people could believe what they wanted.

That was exactly what intrigued me. Japanese visitors identify Tsuru Glover as Butterfly. Glover Garden is commonly called Butterfly Garden. Why does this situation exist? It seemed worthwhile to look for answers. But when I started exploring the history of the opera, I soon ran into a surprising degree of confusion, error, and misinformation, much of which has found its way even into the more serious literature on the subject of Puccini's life and works. In this book, I've tried to give a clear picture of the real background of *Madame Butterfly*, based on a precise chronology of the events from the earliest beginning of the story to the final version of the opera. My research is based on European and Japanese sources and I've tried to give at least a few answers to questions that are still open.

The French novelist Gustave Flaubert speaks about people whose mission in life is to serve as intermediaries. He says such people are like bridges—one uses them as the means to go on. The history of *Madame Butterfly* supplies ample confirmation of that view. The story or parts of the story had to travel by many bridges before they arrived at their common destination, Puccini's opera. The bridges had various sizes and statures: most of them, whether they allowed the passing on of historical events, literary works, or musical airs, were often small, incidental, and sometimes insignificant; a few of them, however, stand out— their works can be enjoyed in their own right. On those bridges one can linger for a while. The most obvious bridge in the context of this story is Pierre Loti's *Madame Chrysanthème*, which, although not really a masterwork, is an important novel. Most other bridges, however, one crosses just to note that they are there, too; their importance lies in the fact that they contribute in some small way to the story's final shape. Their large number and the complicated network they are part of is surprising: so many intakes from so many sides with such different histories finally all converging into the one complex organic entity of Puccini's great opera.

This book focuses on the story of *Madame Butterfly*, the opera and the person, and on their roots in literature and real life. It does not analyze the musical qualities of Puccini's opera. My musical expertise is not sufficient to deal in depth with that aspect, and I would have little to add to the excellent studies on the subject that already exist, particularly those by Mosco Carner and William Ashbrook. I will only refer to musical aspects of the opera where doing so could help explain the history of the composition.

I should like to express my gratitude to all those who have helped me in my research, especially during the years that demanding professional duties left me little time to work on a book. I'd like to mention in particular Dr. Fred Van Poznak, who turned the British Public Record Office upside down to find anything I wanted to know about foreigners in Nagasaki and who made numerous suggestions. And I thank Sakuma Kyoko, Shinagawa Mitsue, and Merial Thomas in Tokyo, and Brian Burke-Gaffney and Midori Matsue in Nagasaki, all of whom assisted me in tracking down and translating Japanese sources and helped me put them in the right context. I especially thank Kuriyama Shigemitsu for his advice on how to interpret Japanese *koseki* (family registers) and Professor Sawada Toshio for supplying me with useful information regarding Mrs. Oyama. I also thank my son Kees van Rij for his stimulating remarks and his contributions to information related to Korea. And I am grateful to Albert Walker, the last survivor of the foreign settlers' families in Nagasaki, for introducing me to their world.

I am grateful also to the very helpful staffs of the British Library in London, the Jardine and Matheson Archives in the library of the University of Cambridge, the Library of Congress in Washington, D.C., and the Bibliothèque-Musée de l'Opéra in Paris, all of whom went out of their way to assist me in finding access to the historical material I needed.

Marie Meyerscough and Ubaldo Gardini were kind enough to carry on new ideas and facts that stimulated my writing. Martin Blakeway and Hara Fujiko supplied me with invaluable sources on the subject of Japonisme; they and Oue Shoji joined me in discovering some of the secrets of old Nagasaki.

I owe particular debts of gratitude to Dr. William Gooddy, who spent many (often early morning) hours reading and correcting the typescript and suggesting numerous improvements, and to W. John Minzinga Zijlstra, who read the complete typescript and proposed a number of changes to improve the presentation of several chapters.

Some of my ideas were born during the very stimulating monthly dinners of the members of the Tokyo Penguin Club. I am grateful for the enthusiasm and the originality of our exchanges and I feel privileged by the warm, personal ties I have maintained with each of them for so many years.

✿  ✿  ✿

The story that eventually became the subject of Puccini's opera is called *Madame Butterfly*. Puccini turned it into the more Italian-sounding *Madama Butterfly*. In this book, the latter name is used when I deal with the opera; when I refer to the short story by John Luther Long, to the play by David Belasco, or to the history of the character in general, I use the name *Madame Butterfly*. As for the Japanese equivalent, this book uses different names according to the context: she is Cho-san in the story of Mrs. Jennie Correll (the first person who mentioned her name), Cho-Cho-san in the novel and the play, and Cio-Cio-san in the opera's libretto.

For other Japanese names throughout this book I follow the traditional style of family name first, then the personal name.

English-language quotations from *Madama Butterfly*'s libretto are taken from William Weaver's *Seven Puccini Librettos* (New York: Norton, 1981), except for passages belonging to its early versions, for which I consulted *Opera Guide 26* (London: John Calder, 1984).

# 1

# The Butterfly Saga:
# O-Taki-San and O-Kiku-San

GIACOMO PUCCINI'S *MADAMA BUTTERFLY* HAS MANY AND
various literary and musical roots. Reduced to its essentials it is,
however, a very simple story. A foreign, in this case an American,
sailor comes to a Japanese treaty port; he arranges to have a
woman and a house for the length of his stay; when his time is

up, he leaves the woman behind, pregnant (but he does not know that) and with a little money; coming back a few years later with his American wife, he discovers the existence of the child, claims it, and prepares to leave again. In despair, the woman kills herself.

This is far from an original story. To the seafaring community of the nineteenth century, the practice of an easy contractual relationship with a poor girl in a Japanese harbor was well known. It had existed for centuries on the minuscule artificial island of Dejima in Nagasaki Bay, where a small trading post of the Netherlands East Indies Company had been allowed to function since 1630, and throughout the Edo period, during which Japan had been otherwise closed off from the rest of the world. As the Japanese had not allowed the Dutch merchants to bring their families with them, there had been on Dejima a lively pattern of hiring Japanese women. This not only met certain requirements of the Dutch residents of Dejima but also permitted the Japanese authorities to know all the details, even the most intimate ones, of what was going on in the daily life of the trading post. To give just one example out of many: Hendrik Doeff, the Dutch governor of Dejima from 1799 until 1817, had two children with women of the Maruyama licensed quarter of Nagasaki; when he returned to the Netherlands, he left money behind for his children's education and for buying them jobs in the future.

Outside of the narrow circle of those who were immediately involved, the practice was not widely known at that time. The Dutch merchants, apart from not belonging to a particularly literary stock, felt no encouragement to write about it. Also, their Calvinistic compatriots in the Netherlands would not have appreciated or tolerated such a liberal life-style. Others would be needed to carry the theme of this peculiar fashion into Western literature and music. One link in the chain was Siebold.

## Siebold's Story

Dr. Philip Franz von Siebold was born in the German city of Würzburg on 16 February 1796. He became a medical doctor and went to Japan as a physician in the service of the Dutch government. He arrived in Dejima on 8 August 1823 for what would be seven years as a doctor for the Dutch factory there. He was twenty-seven years old and had a great eagerness to learn and to teach. He was allowed by the Japanese to give lessons in Western medicine, initially in a private house in Nagasaki and later in the newly built School of Medicine at Narutaki in the northeastern outskirts of the city. He had many students, and patients came from the entire region to consult with him. He performed the first cataract surgery in Japan and introduced the use of the forceps in obstetrics. Moreover he collected an extraordinary treasure of knowledge about Japan's history, geography, nature, and people, which formed the basis of his later books: *Nippon, Flora Japonica*, and *Fauna Japonica*. He regularly shipped thousands of objects and pictures (via the Dutch colonial administration in Batavia, the capital of the Dutch East Indies) to Europe, where they eventually became the foundation of such famous collections of Japanese art and culture as the National Museum of Ethnology in Leiden (in the Netherlands) and the Japanese treasures kept in Munich (Germany). At Dejima he established a botanical garden with some fourteen-hundred different varieties of Japanese plants, and he sent seeds and live plants to Batavia, one of which formed the original stock of what would become the famous Indonesian tea culture.

The young doctor's activities did not stop there. He became acquainted with a Japanese woman, Kusumoto Taki, who worked as a *yujo* (pleasure girl) in the Maruyama district, where she was known as Sonogi.[1] He "married" her according to the usual temporary arrangements. They had a daughter, called Ine or Oine, born on 10 May 1827. Siebold called his temporary wife O-Taki-san (meaning honorable Miss Taki), a name that he immortalized in his *Flora Japonica*, where he names a hydrangea variety after her: *Hydrangea otaksa*.

Siebold was scheduled to return to Europe in 1828 but an incident interrupted his plans. Officials of the shogun discovered that he was in possession of a map of Japan that had been given or sold to him by his friend Takahashi Sakuazemon, an astronomer for the shogun's court in Edo. This was, obviously, a serious offense against the Japanese principles of national security. Siebold was arrested, then confined to his Dejima quarters pending the investigation. During this time, Taki was a constant presence, taking care of the doctor and (we must assume) informing the Japanese police about him. On 2 January 1830, Siebold was officially expelled from Japan. He left Nagasaki with locks of hair from Taki and Oine in his pocket. Back in Europe, he published (in 1832) the first of his books about Japan. His experiences with that country raised much interest in Europe and America at a time when the patience of their political leaders with Japan's centuries-long isolation began to wear out. Commodore Perry learned extensively from Siebold's writings before he sailed to Japan in 1853 to demand on behalf of the United States government the opening up of the country for foreigners and trade.

After his return, Siebold lived in Germany for some thirty years, but stayed in contact with Japan and received letters from Taki, written in broken Dutch. Meanwhile, in 1845, he married Helena von Gagern, with whom he had five children. For his merits, the Dutch government promoted him to the rank of colonel in the Dutch army. When in the late 1850s access to Japan became easier, Siebold managed to be sent out again, this time by the Netherlands Trading Society. He and his son Alexander, who was thirteen, arrived in Nagasaki on 14 August 1859. At the age of sixty-three, he again met his Japanese family. O-Taki-san had remarried twice and was selling kerosene for a living. Oine was now thirty-two years old. She had studied obstetrics and practiced as a midwife. Siebold arranged with Johannes Pompe van Meerdervoort, the very active Dutch doctor of the Dejima settlement, that Oine would follow his classes at the new medical school and the hospital created by him at the request of the Japanese government (the predecessor of the present Nagasaki University Medical School). And so Oine became the first female doctor in Japan and, later on, the chief physician of the daimyo of Uwajima in the island of Shikoku.

For the second time, Siebold stayed in Nagasaki. He again took up his studies of Japan and this time could freely draw maps and write about the country. Bishop George Smith of Victoria, Hong Kong, visited him in 1860 in his house in Inasa at the opposite side of the bay from Nagasaki. With tongue-in-cheek humor he remarks that Herr von Siebold "has had a somewhat varied experience of Japan and the Japanese" but he also notes that "any prejudice against the colonel by portions of his former history appears to have passed away" and he praises Siebold's "friendly intimacy" with the priests of neighboring temples.

Siebold went back to Europe in 1862 and died in Munich on 18 October 1866. The closest witness of his last few days was Alphonse Daudet, who had met him earlier that year in Paris in the company of a young German woman whom Siebold called his niece. Daudet went to see him again in Munich where Siebold, again accompanied by his "niece," showed him the collection he had just offered to the government of Bavaria. In his autobiographical *Contes du Lundi* ("Monday Tales") Daudet conveys the magic of Siebold's profound love of Japan, symbolized by the sixteenth-century Japanese play called *The Blind Emperor.* The doctor had made a translation of the Japanese original to allow his friend Giacomo Meyerbeer to use it for an opera. Since Meyerbeer had died two years before without composing the opera, Siebold wanted to give it to Daudet. Unfortunately, Siebold had not been able to find the manuscript when he died and Daudet never saw it.

Siebold's son Alexander stayed in Japan after his father's departure and was an interpreter for the British legation and later an adviser to Prime Minister Matsukata Masayoshi and Foreign Minister Inoue Kaoru. His younger brother Heinrich also came to Japan, worked for the Austrian legation, and contributed substantially to the Japanese collections of several important German museums.

The story of Dr. von Siebold is of interest because it was one of the first of its kind to become known beyond the circle of those immediately concerned. It was also a prototype of sorts as it contained many of the ingredients of the later novel and play that would be the precursors to Puccini's opera: the marriage of convenience of a Western man and a Japanese bride who used to work as an entertainer; the lighthearted abandonment (Siebold's forced expulsion only came after he already had initiated his return to Europe, planning to leave wife and child behind); the subsequent "real marriage" in Europe, demonstrating that the first marriage was not considered serious or binding; the exchange of letters with the woman in Japan; the return to Japan and concurrent interest in the child. In Siebold's case the return worked out well for his Japanese family but we do not know how well it was received by his European wife.

Siebold's story gained fame and naturally aroused interest and curiosity in Europe and America and even in Japan, largely because of the scientific work he did that was and still is of an importance not matched by any other single foreign explorer of Japan. The private side of Siebold's life in Japan was also well known by insiders but in the Victorian world of his time did not stimulate anybody to use it as a theme for a literary work. Somebody else was needed to bring to the world the emotional aspects of an intimate relationship between a Western man and a Japanese woman.

## Pierre Loti

In July 1885 a vessel of the French navy, the *Triomphante*, sailed into the harbor of Nagasaki for the purpose of an overhaul in the dry dock of the Mitsubishi Shipyard. On board was the lieutenant Julien Marie Viaud, better known as the author Pierre Loti, who besides being a naval officer had an impressive career as the writer of some forty novels, many of which are based on his travel experiences. In his novel *Madame Chrysanthème* (published two years later), as well as in his diaries and correspondence, Loti describes his stay in Nagasaki during the summer of 1885.

In the introductory chapter of the novel, Loti and his friend Yves (in real life his name was Pierre Le Cor, and Loti often refers to him as his "brother") discuss, on the bridge of their ship, Loti's intent to marry "a little yellow-skinned woman with black hair and cat's eyes" and to live with her in "a little paper house." Upon their arrival in Nagasaki on 1 July, they leave the ship to find a certain Mr. Kangourou, recommended to Loti as a "confidential agent for the intercourse of races." Mr. Kangourou arranges a get-together with a Japanese family: mother, aunts, friends, and neighbors (but no father) and of course the fifteen-year-old candidate herself, Mademoiselle Jasmin. The poor girl is rejected and in the embarrassing impasse Yves draws Loti's attention to another girl in the background. She is O-Kiku-san, also

known as Mademoiselle Chrysanthème, about eighteen years old
and the cousin of the rickshaman who has driven Loti to his
appointment. Loti is ready to take her, and Mr. Kangourou
negotiates with the family the usual conditions: a hundred yen
(twenty dollars) per month. On 7 July, the "marriage" is registered and permission for a common household is granted by the
officials of the local police station. Loti and Chrysanthème settle
down on the second floor of a small house on the hill of Ju-Jen-
Ji (today called Juninmachi). The house with paper walls and
sliding panels has previously been inspected by Loti and Yves. It
has a beautiful view of Nagasaki and the harbor and becomes
the point of departure for a large number of picturesque scenes
described by Loti in the novel with precision and great detail.

Loti's time is divided between his tours of duty aboard the
*Triomphante*, periods of leisure in the house, and excursions in
Nagasaki and the countryside, often in the presence of Yves.
Loti, Yves, and Chrysanthème visit teahouses and temples, enjoy
drinks with the bonzes of a nearby temple, and have their pictures taken by the famous Ueno Hikoma, the first commercial
photographer of Japan. Loti does not display feelings of any
depth toward O-Kiku-san, whom he calls "a mere plaything to
laugh at, a little creature of finical forms" and he even considers
a premature "divorce." But he describes her ways of life in detail:
how she plays with her little brother Bambou or does her make-

up or smokes her little pipe or goes through her box where she keeps her scarce belongings. He is vaguely annoyed by the idea that perhaps during his absence something is going on between Yves and Chrysanthème, but when he brings it up, Yves shows sincere surprise because he considers her to be Loti's wife.

Meanwhile, Loti observes Japanese life and paints small pictures of people and situations: a street singer, a funeral, a religious procession, the playing of the samisen (a Japanese lute). He tries to penetrate the history and background of some of the persons he meets. He imagines that Chrysanthème belongs to a higher class than the other girls "married" to foreign sailors; he refers to her "aristocratic distinction" and he finds her mother "vastly superior" to the other "mothers-in-law." Much attention is also given to the elderly couple who live on the ground floor of their house: the landlord Mr. Sato, his wife Mrs. Ume, and their young daughter Oyuki, who is Chrysanthème's inseparable friend. He doesn't forget to keep us informed about the "marriages" of his colleagues of the *Triomphante* and about the assistance given by his "very tall friend" (in real life Louis de Silans) who is not married himself but plays the role of "confidential adviser" of the Japanese wives (the *mousmés*) of the French officers.

A particularly interesting chapter concerns Loti's return to the house after an absence of five days during which he had to stay aboard the ship while it underwent repairs in the Tategami dry dock, a little further down Nagasaki Bay. The *Triomphante* is maneuvered back to her old moorings in the harbor and again within sight of the house. At nightfall Loti and Yves take a sampan to go on land and return home. Loti feels "almost remorseful" for his neglect of Chrysanthème. Meanwhile, she has watched from the house every movement of the ship and, while waiting for his return, decorated the house, lighted the lamps, put fresh flowers in the vases, and donned her best clothes.

On 18 September, Loti has to leave Nagasaki as his ship has been ordered to sail for China. When he announces his departure, O-Kiku-san doesn't seem to be deeply moved. "Something like an expression of sadness passes in her eyes," but that is all. Going home the last evening after the last iced sherbet at the teahouse of the "Indescribable Butterfly," she is "absentminded and silent." When on the day of departure Loti returns to the house for the last time, he finds Chrysanthème sitting on the floor, cheerfully singing and testing the silver dollars he had given her the night before as her due according to the marriage agreement: "With the competent dexterity of an old money-changer she fingers them, turns them over, throws them on the floor, and armed with a little mallet *ad hoc*, rings them vigorously against her ear." Obviously, Chrysanthème was well informed about the recurrence of false silver dollars in Japan and the technique of testing them.

Loti's book had tremendous success. There were twenty-five editions in the five years following its initial publication, and it was translated into several other languages, including English. Apart from the general public interest in exotic stories, typical for the latter half of the nineteenth century, the era of new technologies and new discoveries that brought faraway countries and peoples closer to Europe, there was a strong element of authenticity and genuineness in Loti's writing that seduced and conquered an audience eager to be thrilled by unknown sensations. Whatever can be said about the personality of Pierre Loti, whether he was, as Lesley Blanch puts it in her biography, an "escapist" or, as author and filmmaker Jean Cocteau said, a "painted China goat," whether he was the "sublime illiterate" that French novelist Anatole France called him or a literary genius (he was, after all, a member of the prestigious Académie Française), what is important here is to acknowledge Loti's talent as a writer in presenting a true-to-life picture with only a little touching up, allowing others to see reality through his eyes.

It was that direct view of his "little adventure" in Nagasaki that struck his readers as authentic; they had no doubts about the real facts they were told. Loti really was in Nagasaki in 1885 and he did "marry" a girl of seventeen, whose name was Kane, but his real stay was shorter than that depicted in the novel and the dates were different.[2] The authenticity of the facts is con-

firmed by the private diary Loti kept during his days in Nagasaki
and by his own statement a few years later that he deliberately
took notes on his daily life with Kane because he knew that one
day it could be sold by Calmann-Lévy, his publisher. In his 1988
book *Pierre Loti et l'Extrème Orient* (Pierre Loti and the Far East),
Professor Funaoka reveals how Loti used his diary to create the
novel. Loti's story also appears in a very condensed form in his
undated letter to Juliette Adam of the literary magazine *Nouvelle
Revue*, where he writes: "Last week I got married before the
authorities of this country, my brother Yves and two families
gathered together, with a young girl of seventeen. Her name is
O-Kane-san. In the evening we had a parade with lanterns and a
gala tea. The marriage is valid for as long as the two parties
agree."[3] In another letter to Juliette Adam dated 9 August 1885,
he writes that he left O-Kane-san "without emotion, without
regret" and adds, "it's the end of a little adventure that will never
start again." Nearly twenty years later his friend Claude Farrère
tells us how Loti explained at least one reason why he had no
regrets: "'Kane means money and that name fitted her well,' Loti
said in a resentful way."

   O-Kane-san does not seem to have been the victim of an
unwanted situation. Whether or not she tested her silver dollars
before Loti's departure (Funaoka thinks that the scene was
invented by Loti, but it is authentic and understandable enough

*Photograph of Pierre Loti (right), Pierre Le Cor (left), and O-Kane-san, taken by Ueno Hikoma in Nagasaki in 1885. There is another picture of the two men with another Japanese woman, made on the same occasion, but this one has a caption on the back, written by Loti's daughter-in-law Elise, that confirms the identities. Loti's sailor's hat (absent on the other picture) was probably added by hand at a later time. (Fonds Pierre-Loti-Viaud)*

to be true), she took her pay and went on living a normal life. When Loti returned to Nagasaki in 1900, he heard from Madame Renoncule, his former "mother-in-law," that her daughter Kane had made an advantageous marriage to a businessman from the Nagasaki region. Her only regret was that she had no children. Her mother organized a dinner party for Loti but she thought it wise not to invite her daughter. It all sounds very reasonable.

Rarely has a "little adventure" been so well documented. Besides the written evidence, there is a photograph made by Ueno Hikoma that shows Pierre Loti, Pierre Le Cor, and O-Kane-san. O-Kane-san is seated before the two men with an impassive, indifferent face. Loti describes the photograph in a letter to the young Duchesse de

*The watercolor portrait by Georges Bigot of O-Kane-san, which carries the title* Pierre Loti's Concubine O-Kiku-San. *(Museum "House Number 16," Nagasaki)*

Richelieu, Heinrich Heine's grandniece, which was published with the novel. He subtly explains the identity of the woman in the picture and adds that his novel is not really about Madame Chrysanthème but about "myself, Japan and the effect produced on me by that country." We also have a portrait of O-Kiku-san/O-Kane-san made by Georges Bigot, a French artist who lived in Japan from 1882 until 1899; his watercolor is shown in a little museum called House Number 16 at the bottom of the Minami Yamate hill in Nagasaki and is presented as "Madame Chrysanthème, the concubine of Pierre Loti."[4]

Maybe even more than all the details about Madame Chrysanthème, it is Loti's novel itself that clearly demonstrates its authenticity in the descriptions of Nagasaki, its sites, and the day-to-day scenes. Its indications on locations are very precise and it is clear that the little house where Loti spent a few weeks could hardly have been in another place than where today a stone with an inscription marks the fact.[5] Loti's comments on the "marriage contract" and the "family" show how well aware he was of some of the intricacies of Japanese social conditions. It should be noted, for example, that Loti, unlike many others, recognizes that the poor girls who are temporarily "married" to him and his colleagues are quite distinct from the geisha, who are professional entertainers at a certain artistic level and not necessarily available for sexual relationships. They are also different, he noted, from the *yujo*, the prostitutes of Nagasaki's Maruyama district, though the Maruyama girls would occasionally engage in such contracts as well. Loti refers to that part of town as *le quartier des dames galantes* (the district of the loose ladies), which, when discussed, "causes our mousmés to make a disdainful grimace."

And so it came about that the *Butterfly* theme (but not yet the name) entered Western literature for the first time through Loti's book *Madame Chrysanthème*, published in 1887. Western music soon followed: a few years later, the story was turned into a light opera in four acts, a prologue, and an epilogue by the composer and conductor Charles Prosper André Messager.[6] The first performance took place on 30 January 1893 in the Théâtre Lyrique de la Renaissance in Paris. Messager's *Madame Chrysanthème* largely follows Loti's novel, adapting it where necessary to the scene. Messager understood, however, how difficult it is to produce an operatic work without an intrigue of which there is none in

*O-Kiku-san's portrait by Rossi in the original edition of Loti's* Madame Chrysanthème.

Loti's novel. So he took the only rudimental element of a plot in the book—Loti's unfounded suspicion about a possible sentimental relationship between Yves and Chrysanthème—and he works it out in such a way that Pierre (as he is called here) becomes seriously obsessed and depressed by his misconception. In the epilogue, Pierre finds out that Chrysanthème has been faithful to him after all, then agrees with Yves that "women are women," a conclusion that fits well the operetta style of the work.

Messager had, of course, to adapt Chrysanthème's character to this plot and so she became a more emotional person than she is in the novel and her unhappiness about Pierre's departure is real. One notes also the complete absence of any hint about the money paid to her. Messager's Chrysanthème is moved by love.

As his biographer Henri Février remarks, the musical language of Messager's *Madame Chrysanthème* is written in an "oriental shade, related to the color of *La Princesse Jaune* [The Yellow Princess]," another opera based on a Japanese story made by the

French composer Camille Saint-Saëns, who had been Messager's teacher in Paris. Both works are an example of Japonisme in music.

Messager wrote most of the music of *Madame Chrysanthème* in 1892, in the quiet atmosphere of the countryside Villa d'Este residence of his Italian friend, the publisher Giulio Ricordi. Among the guests was also Giacomo Puccini, who was then working on his opera *Manon Lescaut*. It is impossible not to think that the two composers exchanged some thoughts about their work and the subjects they were dealing with at that time. And although Messager's music is clearly inferior to the product of Puccini's musical genius, this contact between the two men seems to have inspired a few ideas in the heads of Puccini and his librettists when they worked on *Madama Butterfly* some ten years later. That is Messager's modest contribution to the further development of Loti's heroine.

*Who has snapped off this branch?*
*Inside the vase it recaptures*
*a touch of spring.*
*Why argue about whose tree it is?*

KIDO TAKEYOSHI

# 2

## *Japonisme*

AS A SOURCE OF INSPIRATION FOR THE LATER NOVEL, PLAY, AND opera that would focus on the person of Madame Butterfly, Madame Chrysanthème has been of utmost importance. Loti's "little adventure" has without any doubt provided more authentic Japanese details for the *Butterfly* story at all stages of its conception than any other source. Not to be overlooked, however, is the fact that both stories could become so popular in the first

place because of the existence of a predisposition of the public
for things Japanese. The second half of the nineteenth century
saw the peak of the great artistic and fashionable movement
known as "Japonisme," which inundated the hearts and the
minds of a large portion of the public.[1]

## How Did Japonisme Develop?

Japonisme (the French spelling of the word is normally used) is
considerably more than a particular branch of the exoticism that
flourished so abundantly in the nineteenth century after new
technologies opened Western eyes to previously unexplored
worlds. In this context, the "discovery" of Japan had come rather
late, but the excitement that surrounded it was due in part to its
centuries-long isolation; the country had been closed almost her-
metically to the outside world for more than two hundred years.
The only exceptions had been the small Dutch trading post of
Dejima in the harbor of Nagasaki, which received not more than
one or two ships per year, and a handful of Chinese merchants in
the same town. When from 1860 on Japan allowed easier access
to foreigners, there was a sudden and rapidly increasing shift of
exotic interest toward this country that conveyed an image of
originality and purity. Also, unexpectedly, Japan appeared to have
so much new to offer to European art at a time when the latter

was definitely in need of new ideas. As museum director Oshima Seiji wrote (in a catalogue for a 1992 exhibition in Kyoto), ". . . the dynamic effect of Japonisme was due to the combined stimulation of its exotic strangeness and its meaningful content."

The surprise of the encounter is well illustrated by the story told about the French etcher Félix Bracquemond, who in 1856 discovered Hokusai's *manga* (drawings of casual subjects) on the wrapping paper that had been used for shipping some pottery from Japan. When he showed it to a few of his impressionist painter friends, their well-trained eyes recognized the quality of the Japanese work and the answers it contained for some of their own artistic problems. The same anecdote is told about Claude Monet finding Japanese blockprints used as wrapping paper in a grocery shop, and about Alfred Sensier showing accidentally acquired Japanese prints to François Millet and Théodore Rousseau. The brothers Edmond and Jules Goncourt claimed for themselves the initial discovery of Japanese art and its meaning for European artists. Whether true or false, the repetition of these stories shows that Japanese art (or at least the particular branch of Japanese popular pictures that was first discovered) came to Europe at the right time; European artists were searching for ways to move away from the traditional routines celebrated in the official schools and salons.

What attracted European artists in the newly discovered samples of Japanese pictorial art was the originality of its expression: the large, flat, colored areas; the strong contours; the abrupt cutting off of figures by the edge of the picture; the asymmetry of the representation even to the point of leaving the center empty; the strongly diagonal compositions; and the inclination to incorporate nature more as an actor than as an object as was often done in European art.

Many European artists jumped on the novelty, and the use of Japanese models as a repertoire proliferated. European painters began imitating works of Japanese artists or using Japanese motifs such as fans, pots, or kimono in otherwise European subjects. The number of paintings from this period of women (both European and Asian) dressed in kimono and gazing at some small Japanese object are almost too numerous to be counted.[2] Later, Europeans' understanding deepened and they began working creatively in original ways with Japanese techniques and applying Japanese artistic principles in new, autonomous ways. This process was never more clearly described than in the words of Ralph Curtis, who said about James McNeill Whistler, one of the greatest painters in the Japonisme style, that he "grafted on to the tired stump of Europe, the vital shoots of Oriental art." Thus Japonisme, overcoming its exotic phase, became one of the models that stimulated an avant-garde of painters, etchers, sculptors, and architects, among them

Toilette Japonaise, *a painting by Firmin Girard, 1873. The standard ingredients one finds in many works of the period of Japonisme, including Puccini's* Madama Butterfly, *are already in place in this painting: the kimono, lanterns, flowers, fans, a screen, a samisen, and so on. (Museo de Ponce, Puerto Rico)*

Édouard Manet, Claude Monet, Edgar Degas, Henri Toulouse-Lautrec, Pierre Bonnard, Édouard Vuillard, Vincent van Gogh, James McNeill Whistler, Pierre Puvis de Chavannes, Félix Bracquemond, Hendrik Breitner, Willem de Zwart, Auguste Rodin, Paul Hankar, and Otto Wagner.

There is yet another element that explains the European

readiness to receive lessons from Japanese artistic mastery, in particular in the fields of applied arts and industrial design. Mass production of practical objects for use in daily life in the industrial age had suffered from a lack of creative design; the result was the generalization of industrial products and the loss of any kind of harmonic relationship between form and decoration. Starting in the middle of the nineteenth century, movements such as Arts and Crafts in England and *Libre Esthétique* ("Free Aesthetics") in Belgium were born out of the need for better decorative designing. The British designer Christopher Dresser played a major role in conveying to European craft and industry principles of Japanese aesthetics and thus contributed much to the Victorian craze for Japanese art and decoration in England.

Through a spillover effect on schools such as the Art Nouveau movement (so named for the "Salon de l'Art Nouveau" that the art dealer Samuel Bing opened in Paris in 1895), this later form of Japonisme spread across Europe through a variety of disciplines and styles: the architect Charles Rennie Mackintosh in Glasgow; the glass artist Emile Gallé in Nancy; and Otto Wagner's Secession movement in Vienna, represented by Gustav Klimt, Joseph Hoffman, and Kolo Moser. Belgian architecture (Victor Horta) and Dutch design (the Rosenburg faience of The Hague) followed the movement with many original contributions. Tiffany and Co. in New York closed the circle by employ-

ing Japanese craftsmen for the manufacturing of its Art Nouveau objects by the end of the century.

The word "Japonisme" thus became a synonym for the inte-
gration of principles of Japanese design into Western art. The
word "Japonaiserie," on the other hand, reflects an interest in
Japanese styles in a more superficial way—because of their exotic
and fashionable qualities. The entire field of craft and industrial
design is often much closer to Japonaiserie than to Japonisme,
but a clear distinction is not always possible. The same idea
applies to music; the use of the pentatonic scale (by several
European composers of the nineteenth century) is a form of
Japonisme, whereas the simple use of the Japanese national
anthem (as Puccini did in *Madama Butterfly*) would be an example
of Japonaiserie.

## Japonisme's Prevalence in the 1800s

European motives to use Japanese models were enhanced by a
strong push from the Japanese side, though the latter had entirely different reasons, strongly motivated by economic and political considerations. Since the 1850s, Japan had enacted treaties
with the United States and most European countries that
allowed and promoted free trade through treaty ports and created concessions in those ports where foreigners could settle out-

side of Japanese jurisdiction. Diplomatic missions were established and foreign merchants arrived, soon followed by travelers, artists, and collectors. The new government, in place in Tokyo after the 1868 coup of the Western clans against the shogunate (the Meiji Restoration), quickly grasped the interest of developing, for a number of reasons, the export of Japanese art.

When Japan opened up to the world after having been isolated for over two hundred years, it had to catch up very quickly with the industrialized nations to be able to defend its interests internationally. First of all it needed to understand and adopt the latest state of the art in Western government, industry, and banking. Japanese missions traveled the world to learn about Western methods and buy Western technologies. Exports were necessary to earn the funds needed for buying foreign goods, services, and knowledge. Japanese art and craft were at the time among the most readily available commodities and their exports were actively pursued by Japanese officials and dealers.

Japan also had strong political motives for the export of its traditional art. The situation of the treaty ports, with their exclusive foreign concessions, extraterritoriality, consular jurisdiction, and internationally controlled customs tariffs, implied an intolerable interference with Japanese sovereignty. After the 1860s, Japan's foreign policy aimed at the revision and the abolition of the "unequal treaties." Consecutive Japanese governments had the conviction that a high level of worldwide respectability and trust was needed to convince other countries to agree to abolish the treaties and reestablish Japanese sovereignty everywhere in Japan. This objective was to be pursued by both Japan's adoption of Western legal and political systems as well as an outspokenly Western life-style, and the promotion of a Japanese image that would show that, like European countries, it linked a modern present to a prestigious, traditional past of a high cultural level and thus clearly belonged to another class than the many colonialized countries of Asia and Africa.[3]

Since the Meiji Restoration, the central government was in control of this policy. A state company was created in 1874 with the purpose of organizing and controlling the exports of Japanese art and was active until 1891, when its existence was no longer felt to be relevant for the government's objectives. But during this short period many useful tasks were accomplished: the company played an important role in guaranteeing and assuring short-term delivery for ordered goods (thus distinguishing Japanese exports favorably from those of China and other Asian countries), organizing outgoing trade missions, and coordinating Japanese participation in international trade and industry fairs. After the late 1860s, there was not a major international exhibition in Europe or America without a massive Japanese presence. Along with these abundant shows of Japanese paintings, ceramics, enamels, lacquerware, silk, bamboo, woodworks, and books, an enormous trade activity developed both at the high and the low ends of the market. Mass exports flourished. Diplomats and visitors acquired treasures for themselves that later on would often make their way, through auctions or otherwise, to public collections. Museums, particularly in France, Germany, Austria, the Netherlands, and the United Kingdom, made large purchases for their Japanese art departments. Art dealers like the brothers Samuel and Auguste Bing, Wakai and Hayashi in Paris, and Arthur Lasenby Liberty in London (who would leave his name to the Liberty style in fabrics and domestic objects) thrived on the trade in Japanese art.

## JAPONISME IN LATE-1800S MUSIC AND THEATER

There is no doubt that Japonisme had its main impact in the fields of painting, sculpture, and architecture, but it had also some influence in music. As the music critic Michel Fleury remarks, "The assimilation by western music of elements borrowed from the Asian or Arab East should be seen in parallel with the influence of Japanese painting on Whistler or Manet." The process of adoption of this type of exoticism is perhaps less clearly visible because Japanese music, once experienced, turned out to be less abundantly useful for Western music than

Japanese art was for Western art. Nevertheless, even if less evident, there is without doubt Japonisme in music.

The oldest example is the simple and playful *La Princesse Jaune*, made in 1872 by the French composer Camille Saint-Saëns. Saint-Saëns himself declared that at the time he hardly could have avoided a Japanese subject because "people talked about nothing else but Japan." The story takes place in the Netherlands and concerns Kornélis, a Dutch doctor (generally believed to be inspired by Siebold), the doctor's cousin Léna, who is in love with him, and the image of a Japanese woman, the Yellow Princess, who emerges from her screen to come to life in the shape of Léna. There is a passionate love song from Kornélis and an outburst of jealousy from Léna before things become normal again and the doctor and his cousin embrace each other in a happy ending. The libretto has some Japanese lines and reveals the common fantasies about the peaceful, happy life of Japanese women. The music in some places uses pentatonic scales, apparently for the first time ever in European music. Today, Saint-Saëns's simple opera is no longer performed, but has its place in history as the first Western musical work with a Japanese theme and using a Japanese musical technique; it could become a decisive link in the chain between original Japanese elements and Western music because of the influence of Saint-Saëns on other composers such as Messager, Pietro Mascagni, and Claude

Debussy, who in various ways were sources of inspiration for Puccini.

Pietro Mascagni's *Iris* (1898) deserves a special mention in this context not only because of the composer's link with Saint-Saëns (whose intimate friend Antonio Bazzini later became Mascagni's and Puccini's composition teacher at the Milan Conservatory) but also for the reason that its libretto was written by Puccini's librettist Luigi Illica. The Iris of the opera is a Japanese heroine exploited by a rich Japanese suitor (Osaka) who tries, in vain, to conquer her with the assistance of a middleman (Kyoto). Iris has to confront her blind father who, selfishly, claims her constant attention and repudiates her when he mistakenly thinks she has abandoned him by selling herself to a Yoshiwara teahouse; in reality she has been abducted there by Osaka and Kyoto. When she sees no other way out of her misery, she commits suicide by throwing herself out of a window. The simplicity and triviality of this story are partly compensated by the elaboration of the main characters and the exalted mysticism of Iris's adoration of the sun. There are a few traces of Japanese music in the score, but on the whole it is an Italian opera based on a Japanese story. As musical historian Mosco Carner remarks, Mascagni's excursion into legendary Japan "may well have kindled in Puccini the desire to try his hand at a similar subject" as the one handled by his old rival. Puccini's feelings about *Iris* were certainly mixed. He admired Mascagni's instrumentation but thought that the opera had "a defect at origin: action that is uninteresting and pines and fades away for three acts." Nevertheless there are in Puccini's *Madama Butterfly* clear reminiscences of Mascagni's *Iris*, for example in the scenes of the vigil and the preparation of the suicide.

At the extreme end of the popularization of things Japanese, we find the world of the theater: light comedies, operettas, musical comedies, vaudeville, and even circuses based on Japanese subjects. This is obviously all Japonaiserie, not so much a style as a fashion that reflects the ongoing fascination with Japan. Going through old theater books, I found a large concentration of such lighthearted works, mostly produced in France, in the second half of the 1870s with titles such as *La Japonaise* (music by Emile Jonas), *La Troupe Japonaise de Yeddo*, *Le Tour du Japon*, *Kisoko*, *Kosiki* (music by Charles Lecocq), *La Belle Saïnara*, and *Yedda*. From the 1880s, there are fewer musical works based on a Japanese theme, but three are noteworthy: *La Japonaise* (another one, this time with music by Louis Varney), *La Marchande de Sourires*, a musical play by Judith Gautier, and the famous musical comedy *The Mikado*. The 1890s reveal a new harvest of Japanese ballets (*Papa Chrysanthème*) and musical comedies such as Messager's *Madame Chrysanthème*, Sidney Jones's *The Geisha*, and *Mé-Na-Ka* (music by Gaston Serpette). At the turn of the century, the Japanese theater group of

Kawakami Sadayakko and Otojiro toured Europe with its Japanese plays. Most of these should not be taken too seriously but a few deserve a closer look because of the impact they had in their time.

The theme, already used by Saint-Saëns, of happy Japanese women selling their smiles is taken up again by Judith Gautier (also known as Judith Walter, her early pen name, or Judith Mendès, a name she took during her short-lived marriage to French poet and writer Catulle Mendès). She was the daughter of the French poet Théophile Gautier and the actress Ernesta Grisi. Like her father, she was a great admirer of everything coming from the Far East. In her youth (she was born in 1846), she studied Chinese grammar, astrology, and magic with a Chinese called Tin Tun Ling who in the world of the Parisian artists was commonly called "le Chinois de Théophile Gautier." At just seventeen years of age, she published *The Book of Jade* and *The Imperial Dragon*.[4] When she and Catulle Mendès went to see Richard Wagner on their honeymoon in 1866, the latter fell immediately in love with her (their correspondence suggests that she was his mistress) and she became the promoter of his music in France.

This remarkable and gifted woman was fascinated by Japan. In 1885 she published a French translation of old Japanese poems under the title *Poèmes de la Libellule* (Poems of the Dragonfly), and she wrote several plays on Japanese themes, including *La*

*Marchande de Sourires* (The Woman Selling Her Smiles), which was performed for the first time in 1888 in Paris with music by Benedictus (a mediocre composer with whom she lived at that time). She dedicated this work to the Marquis Saionji Kimmochi, a court noble, diplomat, and later prime minister of Japan, who was then the Japanese minister in Paris.

The play is the story of a boy, Iwashita, whose mother dies after her husband Yamato repudiates her in favor of his mistress Coeur de Rubis. The mistress then steals Yamato's money and gives it to her lover, Simabara. Then she burns Yamato's house and orders Simabara to kill him. The nurse, Tika, is about to save Iwashita when the Prince of Maeda enters. Tika tells him the sad story and asks him to help the child. The Prince adopts the child but sends the nurse away. Twenty years later, Iwashita falls in love with a woman called Fleur de Roseau who turns out to be the daughter of Coeur de Rubis and Simabara. Yamato (who managed to escape his killer) and Tika both return to the same place and recognize Coeur de Rubis. They urge the reluctant Iwashita to kill the woman who caused death and misery to his family, but Coeur de Rubis repents, then commits suicide with a dagger. She asks her daughter to marry Iwashita and dies after her past crimes have been forgiven by all.

Some of the scenes of this melodrama show a remarkable likeness with a few scenes of Puccini's *Madama Butterfly*. The meeting on the road of Tika and the child Imashita with the Prince of Maeda forms the most striking example, as it recalls Butterfly's fantasy of meeting the emperor on the road and showing him her son Dolore. After leaving Iwashita with the Prince, Tika earns her living by playing the samisen and singing in the street, just as Butterfly tells Sharpless in the opera that she will do if Pinkerton does not come back. As Puccini's librettist Luigi Illica was familiar with the work of Judith Gautier, it is very probable that he had this scene in mind when he wrote the outline for the corresponding scene in act 2 of Puccini's opera. Puccini himself could not have seen *La Marchande de Sourires,* which was only performed in Paris in 1888, a year during which he did not travel to Paris.

What Puccini might have seen, however, is Sidney Jones's *The Geisha,* a musical comedy first performed in London in 1896 with text by Owen Hall and lyrics by Harry Greenbank. A French adaptation by Clairville, Mars, and Lemaire was put on the stage in Paris late in 1898, but after a limited number of performances it failed to seduce its public, unlike the English original, which had many reruns. Given Puccini's passion for the theater, he could have seen the French version when he visited Paris in January 1899 or the English version at any time during one of his visits to London. But in any case, it is not likely that the routine themes of this comedy—the expectations foreign sailors have of samisen-playing geishas in a "happy Japan"—would have made a profound and long-lasting impression upon him.

A more noteworthy example of Japonaiserie is *The Mikado*, a musical comedy in two acts from the famous British partnership of William Schwenck Gilbert and Arthur Seymour Sullivan. This work was first performed in 1885 in the London Savoy Theatre. As one critic has pointed out, Sullivan had rediscovered and wished to rehabilitate a long-lost English style of music, and did so in the madrigal of this "opera" in Japonaiserie style.[5] This is a case of artistic renewal not based on Japanese principles but just dressed up in Japanese clothes (in a literal sense, as well: the dresses used in London were made of Japanese fabric and ordered from Liberty, and some were even authentic and two hundred years old). *The Mikado*'s Japanese appearance was timely as the premiere coincided with the exhibition of the Japanese Village in Knightsbridge. While the story is an entirely English satire merely set in a Japanese environment, it is interesting to note the use of a pentatonic scale and a Japanese text: the Japanese army's war song "Miya sama" for which Sullivan acquired words and music through the British traveler Arthur Diósy.[6] The same theme was used later by Puccini, who knew of *The Mikado* and had an English piano score from it.[7] Puccini had briefly met Sullivan in London in 1896, a year during which *The Mikado* was still being performed.

*Postcard photograph of the Japanese actress Sadayakko taken during the European tour she made with her husband, Kawakami Otojiro, around 1900.*

Pure Japonaiserie was also presented in the shows *The Geisha and the Knight, Kesa,* and *The Shogun,* performed by Kawakami Otojiro's Japanese pantomime theater. Otojiro's wife, Sadayakko, played major parts in the shows. They came at least twice to Europe during the years 1900 to 1902. Their plays, described as "vivid, life-like realism," would be without relevance for our subject except that we know Puccini went to Milan to meet Sadayakko in 1902; he must have seen at least some of the shows at that time. Perhaps the opening scene of *The Geisha and the Knight,* with its abundance of cherry blossoms, inspired *Madama Butterfly*'s flower scene of act 2, for which there is no example in any of the other sources.

What are the sources of Japonisme in *Madama Butterfly*? It is tempting to speculate about the Japanese origin of the pentatonic scales used by Puccini. As they were introduced in Europe by Saint-Saëns, it could well be that their use in European music

had been carried by his close friend Antonio Bazzini to the
Milan Conservatory and there gratefully adopted by Pietro
Mascagni and Giacomo Puccini, his students. It is also possible
that Puccini got the idea from André Messager, who had been a
student of Saint-Saëns. Puccini had met him in 1892 (when
Messager was working on *Madame Chrysanthème*), and they worked
closely together in 1903 on the Paris production of *Tosca*, con-
ducted by Messager. This seems the more likely as Mosco Carner
has shown that at least two of *Madama Butterfly*'s Japanese themes
were previously used by Messager in *Madame Chrysanthème*.[8]

Also possible is the assumption that Puccini borrowed his
pentatonic scales from Claude Debussy, who was himself indebted to Saint-Saëns for their use. Debussy had great admiration for
Saint-Saëns and was inspired by him for a number of his works.
Debussy used pentatonic scales in many compositions, including
*L'Enfant Prodigue* (1884) and *Pelléas et Mélisande* (1902). Puccini
admired Debussy (a feeling that was not really reciprocated),
possessed many scores of Debussy's music, and actually met him
in 1903, when he worked on *Madama Butterfly*. Most of all, however, the fact that Puccini directly adopted two ideas from *Pelléas*
for *Madama Butterfly* proves how much he owes to Debussy's harmonic and orchestral innovation.[9]

# Japonisme in the 1900s

Even if it continued to inspire Western artists, Japonisme as a style had outlived itself by the early 1900s. A new view of Japanese art was breaking through around the turn of the century, a view that recognized the existence and importance of an ancient art in Japan only remotely or not at all related to the popular art of the blockprints and the utensils of the nineteenth century. Japanese popular art had conveyed many new and useful ideas to a European avant-garde, but the public had now lost much of its interest. Also, the rise of Japan to the level of a modern world power altered its image abroad, and its successful military action against China between 1894 and 1895 sent a chill throughout the world. The country was no longer viewed as having "that most divine sweetness of disposition which . . . places Japan in these respects higher than any other nation . . ." as the poet Sir Edwin Arnold wrote in 1891. That same year, the scholar Basil Hall Chamberlain observed that "the educated Japanese have done with their past. They want to be somebody else and something else than what they have been and still partly are."

By the early 1900s, Japonisme began to fade, although its impact had been so strong that it would only gradually disappear. "Once the movement had started, the swarm of amateurs followed," wrote the critic Ernest Chesnau in 1878, adding, "It is no longer a fashion, it is a craze, it is an insanity." In particular, the craze lingered on in the form of popular, intrigued curiosity about Japan, one that had been nurtured by an entire generation of artists, designers, travelers, writers, and musicians. Those feelings would not disappear so soon. Whatever Puccini's sources were, it is clear that *Madama Butterfly* was a product of Japonisme.

*Toward the end of the day I stopped
at a small tea house, where a young
woman named Butterfly handed me
a small piece of white silk and asked
me to write a poem choosing her
name as the subject.*

BASHO MATSUO

# 3

# The Butterfly Saga: Cho-Cho-San

THE STORY OF MADAME BUTTERFLY (O-CHO-SAN OR CHO-Cho-san) begins, as did O-Kiku-san's, in Nagasaki. In 1892 a couple of American missionaries, Dr. Irvin H. Correll of the American Methodist Mission and his wife Sarah Jane (commonly called Jennie), arrived in that city, where Dr. Correll became the headmaster of the Chinzei Gakkan school for boys for a period of two years.[1] They remained in Nagasaki for missionary work and teaching until 1897, when they returned to America for home leave. During their years in Nagasaki, the couple lived in House Number 6 on Higashi Yamate (East Hill), a part of the foreign concession (the other parts being Minami Yamate, or South Hill, and Dejima, the former Dutch settlement).

While living in Nagasaki, Jennie heard of the event that would later become the story of Madame Butterfly. At the time of her return to Philadelphia in 1897, Jennie talked about it to her brother John Luther Long, a lawyer with literary aspirations who lived in that city. Jennie was twelve years older than her brother but in spite of this large difference in age the two had a very close relationship and a mutual admiration. From Japan Jennie sent letters to her brother that unfortunately have disappeared but must have contributed to the knowledge of daily life in Japan that John Luther displayed in his writings. During her stay at his house, Jennie told John Luther the story of the "teahouse girl" whom she called Cho-san. Her brother wrote a short story based on Jennie's information and according to Jennie asked her to mark in the margin the places where she found anything "not true to the life" so that he could revise it. The story was published a few months later.

This is the real genesis of the story. Unfortunately, Jennie

Correll was the only living witness when in a series of lectures she gave in Japan in 1931 she reveals exactly what she told her brother in 1897, so we have to rely largely on her testimony, which is not impeccable. There are, as far as I know, three versions of Jennie's presentation of the story, and because it was told thirty-four years after she first mentioned it to her brother (and an even longer time since she heard it herself), some caution is warranted as to what exactly Jennie knew about it originally. The three versions are based on press reports concerning two talks she gave on 12 March and 13 March 1931 in Tokyo:

> 1. An article in the *Japan Times* of 15 March 1931;

> 2. An article in the *Japan Magazine* 21 (1931), which is approximately the same as the above but revised by Jennie; and

> 3. An article in the Japanese-language newspaper *Jiji Shimpo* of 13 March 1931.

The article in *Jiji Shimpo* specifically refers to a talk given on the day before, 12 March, whereas the articles in the *Japan Times* and the *Japan Magazine* indicate that the talk was given on 13 March. Below I've reprinted some of the text from the *Japan Magazine*, because it was revised by Mrs. Correll herself. The follow-

ing quotations are limited to the part of her talks where she
deals with the story itself.

> On the hill opposite ours lived a tea-house girl; her
> name was Cho-san, Miss Butterfly. She was so sweet
> and delicate that everyone was in love with her. In
> time we learned that she had a lover. That was not
> so strange, for all tea-house girls have lovers, if they
> can get and hold them. Cho-san's young man was
> quite nice, but very temperamental, of a moody,
> lonely disposition.
>
> One evening there was quite a sensation when it
> was learned that poor little Cho-san, and her baby,
> had been deserted. The man had promised to
> return at a certain time; had even arranged a signal
> so that Cho-san would know when his ship had
> come in; but the little girl-wife awaited that signal
> in vain. Many an hour and many a long night did
> she peer from her shoji over the lovely harbour, but
> to no purpose: he never returned.

The *Jiji Shimpo* version is much shorter than the above and
shows significant variations. As these differences originate in a
separate talk on another day, they deserve to be emphasized. The
story, as literally translated as possible, runs like this:

I became involved in Madame Butterfly's main
character, O-Cho-san, 34 years ago; I was for the
first time in Nagasaki with my husband Dr. Correll
for the purpose of founding Chinzei Gakkuin;
from my usual shopkeeper I heard the story about
the sorrowful death of O-Cho-san. This story of
O-Cho-san engraved a strong impression in the
deepest of my feelings.

## John Luther Long's Adaptation

In Chapter 5, I will return to some of these differences to exam-
ine what can be deduced from them about the real models of the
story.[2] At this point, however, it is more relevant to look at what
John Luther Long did with his sister's information. In her "reve-
lation" of 1931 (that is the word she uses in her talks) about
what happened in 1897, Jennie states that she "happened to tell"
(the same expression occurs in both the English and Japanese
versions) the story to her brother and that immediately the spirit
of the "literary artist" was aroused in him. He worked, she says,
on a short story all through the following night and showed her
the result the next day, asking her for her suggestions with a view
toward correcting anything that would not be authentic ("true to
the life," as Jennie put it). In her lectures, Jennie didn't reveal

whether she suggested any changes; she just remembers how
amazed she was at the "beautifully pathetic story" her brother
had made.

This was the short story published soon afterward in the January 1898 issue of the *Century Illustrated Monthly Magazine*.[3] John
Luther Long (who published other short stories with titles such
as "Miss Cherryblossom in Tokyo," "A Gentleman of Japan and
a Lady," and "Purple Eyes") was not a great writer but his lack of
talent was compensated to an extent by his eagerness to be correct on all details (perhaps not so surprising given that he was a
lawyer). As a mediocre author, he ostensibly preferred to borrow
his facts from trustworthy sources in order to compose an
authentic and convincing narrative, rather than invent them himself. His meticulousness on such borrowed details clearly shows
up in the short story, which runs along the following lines:

Aboard his ship that is about to arrive in Nagasaki, Lieutenant Pinkerton of the United States Navy, just coming from
the Mediterranean, and his friend Sayre discuss Sayre's suggestion that Pinkerton might get himself married in Japan, advice
that Pinkerton follows with the help of the marriage broker
Goro. His "wife" Cho-Cho-san, or Madame Butterfly, is forced
by Pinkerton to accept that neither her relatives nor her ancestors will be welcome at their house (which has been rented with
the assistance of Goro on the Higashi Hill for 999 years).

Because of this she is disowned by the members of her family, who had initially approved her contract (the nature and price of which she understands) with Pinkerton. As a result of Pinkerton's refusal of both "living and dead" ancestors, Butterfly secretly starts seeing the missionary on the opposite hill and considers conversion to Christianity.

After Pinkerton's departure, Butterfly has his baby. She, the maid Suzuki, and the little boy Trouble go on living in the same house with some money he left behind. We learn that Trouble is a temporary name that later on may be changed to Joy. Most of the ensuing story consists of dialogues between the two women about their situation (which is critical and might force Butterfly to become a street singer with her samisen, to earn some money) and about Pinkerton's possible return; between Butterfly and Goro about another "marriage" with a rich Japanese (which she refuses); between Butterfly and the matrimonial candidate himself, Prince Yamadori (whom she politely ridicules and then throws out); and between Butterfly and the American vice-consul Sharpless (whom she visits twice to get certainty about her situation), to whom she confesses that, initially, she meant to get married "for a while" to procure food and clothing to her needy grandmother and who kindly advises her to accept Yamadori's offer. Sharpless also takes it upon himself to inform Pinkerton about the child.

MADAME BUTTERFLY

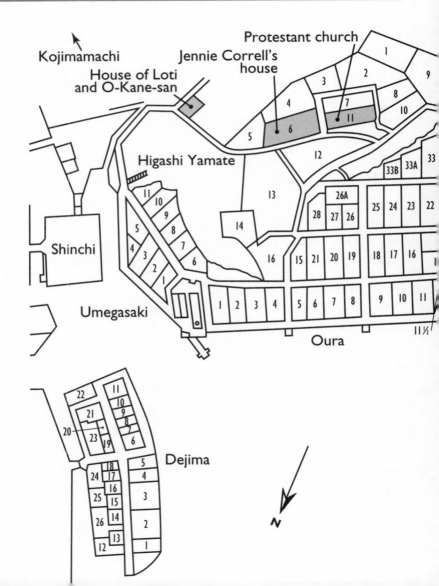

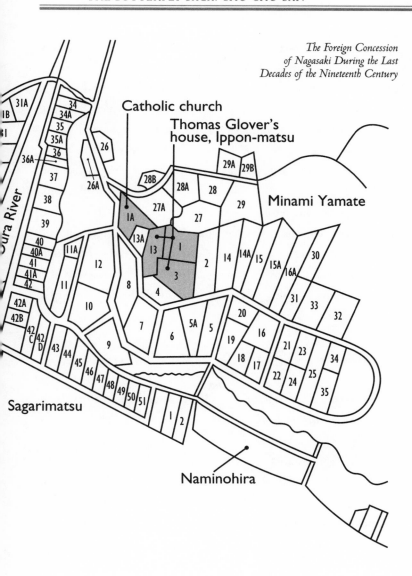

*The Foreign Concession*
*of Nagasaki During the Last*
*Decades of the Nineteenth Century*

Catholic church

Thomas Glover's
house, Ippon-matsu

Minami Yamate

Dura River

Sagarimatsu

Naminohira

Eventually Pinkerton's ship returns (on 17 September) and the women prepare the house and themselves for his welcome, then wait days and nights in vain. One day Butterfly discovers Pinkerton on the deck of a passenger steamer, which had just arrived, with a blond woman on his arm. The next day Pinkerton's ship leaves again (for China, so Sharpless tells her). A woman, Pinkerton's wife Adelaide, arrives and wishes to take the baby with her. Butterfly, who so far has believed Pinkerton's promises about his return (particularly because he didn't divorce her when he left the first time) now understands the reality of her situation. She tries to commit suicide (as her father had done in the past) but stops in time. When Adelaide comes to the house the next morning to take possession of the child, the two women and the baby are gone.

## Comparisons between Loti's and Long's Story

Obviously, nearly all of the elements in Long's story have been borrowed from Loti: the naval officer; the initial discussion with Sayre (Loti's Yves); the marriage broker Goro (Loti's Kangourou), eager to satisfy his customer and earn his fee; the maid Suzuki (Loti's Oyuki); the house on the hill with the paper walls, sliding screens, and locks; the initial "look-at" meeting with the candidate bride; the contract and the price paid for the girl's ser-

vices; the arrival of the family and the drinks; the importance of
the ancestors; Pinkerton's sarcasms about the Japanese; the
notion of the "opposite hill"; the street singer; the possibility of
a divorce; and the return of the ship and the decoration of the
house. Also, there are countless other small details that are similar: Butterfly being called a "plaything" by Adelaide, the samisen,
the tobacco box, the photographs, Yamadori's appearance as a
"ready-made clothier," Butterfly's father having been a samurai,
Butterfly's ways of handling the baby (recalling Chrysanthème's
ways with her baby brother Bambou), the steep roads up and
down the hill, the expectation that Pinkerton will be sent to China after Japan, and even the date of that event—17 September.
All this and more comes from Loti. As for the new characters in
Long's story, Sharpless takes over the role of the friendly adviser
that in Loti's novel is shared by Yves and their "very tall friend."
Only Adelaide and Yamadori are original creations from Long,
the former appearing to be an arrogant upper-middle-class
woman and the latter a Westernized aristocrat, "one of the modern pensioned princes of Japan, a desirable matrimonial article."

In spite of his limited talents Long managed to change some
of the persons he borrowed from Loti into new characters and
to introduce a plot. In particular his Madame Butterfly is a much
more interesting person than Madame Chrysanthème (who,
admittedly, is in Loti's eyes not even the main character of his

novel). Long's Cho-Cho-san, in spite of the unfortunate southern U.S. accent she speaks, is a lively mixture of naiveté and
straightforwardness. She is not very bright (Long refers to her
"little unused frivolous mind") and she is easily misled, not distinguishing wit from reality. She has, however, strong convictions
on a few fundamental issues. She knows that she is being paid a
price for her contract but she assumes Pinkerton knows that subsequently she fell in love with him and that, since he promised to
come back and (more importantly) did not divorce her when he
left but instead gave her money for her survival, she can safely
consider herself as being married in the Western manner. Her
verification with Sharpless of American divorce procedures confirms her assessment of the situation.

Butterfly's religion remains the usual Japanese mixture of
Shinto and Buddhism (like Madame Chrysanthème's), but since
her family did in fact cast her out she is uncertain about the
accessibility of the Japanese gods and sees Christianity as a possible alternative, the more so as it gives her an insight into what
her "husband's" moral attitudes should be. The missionary's
remark about a possible conversion at the eleventh hour allows
her to postpone this option. When finally her world falls apart,
she chooses a Japanese solution: to die when she cannot live with
honor any longer. Halfway through she stops, however, because
she remembers something Pinkerton taught her: to live. In the

end, Butterfly's decision to disappear with the child is a revenge of great dignity.

The other main character of the story, Lieutenant B. F. Pinkerton of the U.S. Navy, who just arrived from the Mediterranean, is obviously modeled on Pierre Loti, a lieutenant in the French Navy, who had just come from Toulon, the main French marine base in the Mediterranean. His direct appearance in the story hardly covers more than four columns out of a total of thirty-six in the *Century Magazine*, but his central role is felt from beginning to end through the comments others make about him. His personality is different, however: Loti is a sensitive man who watches Japan with an attitude somewhere between disappointment with a Japan that changes quickly and will soon be like any other country and racially colored condescension about what he perceives as ridiculous patterns of behavior of some Japanese. But sometimes he is touched by details that he senses as authentically human. He remains, however, a cool and keen observer who does not interfere in anybody's ways of life. Pinkerton is a shallow egotist who feels no need whatsoever to understand Japan. He waves aside what he doesn't like and tries to mold his temporary arrangements in a way that is most convenient for himself without paying attention to feelings of others. He is also an arrogant practical joker and his jokes are crude and thoughtless. And where Loti comes back to say good-bye to Chrysanthème before he leaves, Pinkerton, when he returns to Nagasaki, sends his wife to pick up the baby because he doesn't want to be confronted with Butterfly. He is a repulsive character, a little worse than strictly necessary for explaining a situation that, after all, was not an exceptional one at that time and place.

## How Authentic Is Long's Story?

Throughout the story, small details show Long's amazingly accurate knowledge of Japanese life, customs, and history. To give a few examples: the "lease" of the house was in reality a right of superficies for 999 years created by Japanese law specially for the benefit of foreigners living outside the concessions; the changing of names during a lifetime was still common use in Japan when the Corrells lived there; Butterfly's samurai father's suicide at Jokoji (a small mistake; the name of the place is Jokomyoji) during the Satsuma rebellion could really have been a sacrifice "at the side of the Emperor" as Long writes, because although the rebellion was directed against the legitimate government of Japan, its leader Saigo Takamori always maintained that he intended to protect the emperor against the government in Tokyo; the marriage for money was decided by Butterfly herself (and only subsequently approved by the family) because women

*The Yokohama courtesan Kiyu committing suicide in the* jigai *manner of women of the samurai class. (Drawing by Yoshitoshi Tsukioka)*

of the samurai class could not be sold by their family but they could sell themselves; and finally the act of *jigai,* suicide by a dagger or short sword piercing the neck, was reserved for women of the samurai class to which, in Long's story, Butterfly belongs.

Another interesting example of Long's profound knowledge of Japan is the link he makes between Pinkerton's decision to refuse to allow Butterfly to honor her ancestors and Butterfly's option to change her religion. In Japan the well-being of the living depends on the care given to the dead, including household rites for the ancestors; the neglect of such rites will provoke the malevolence of their spirits toward the living who are guilty of such neglect and will fatally lead to their misfortune; it is to avoid such misfortune that Butterfly is ready to adopt the faith of the Christian missionary as an alternative way of protection.

*View of Minami Yamate seen from Higashi Yamate, as it must have looked around 1870. In the center is Thomas Glover's house Ippon-matsu and to the left the Catholic Church. (Bauduin Collection)*

Long probably didn't want to link such an opportunistic approach toward religion to the Methodist persuasion of the Longs and the Corrells, so he preferred to let Madame Butterfly, for the comfort of her soul, go to receive the teachings of the missionary on the "opposite hill": since Pinkerton's house in his story is explicitly located on Higashi Yamate, the missionary in question could not be anybody other than the priest of the

Catholic Church of the 26 Martyrs on the opposite Minami Yamate hill, operating under the authority of Monseigneur Cousin, the bishop of Kyushu.

Apart from being indebted to Loti and his sister Jennie, Long must also have received much of his detailed knowledge from his reading of some of the widely known authors on Japan that existed in his time. There is, for instance, a remarkable likeness between his description of Butterfly's preparations for her intended suicide, with her quiet preliminaries, makeup, and prayers, and the widespread story of the *jigai* committed in 1895 by the widow of a Lieutenant Asada. The expression used by Long for the way Butterfly looks at her sword ("affectionately") is used for the same purpose in A. B. Mitford's report on a famous suicide case that took place in 1868 and was published a year later.[4]

## Evolution of the Story

Why did Long want to publish the short story? His motivations were probably not limited to just the desire to write a realistic and popular story. Neither Jennie Correll, with her missionary idealism, nor John Luther Long, with his literary ambitions, could have been interested in just exposing one individual case of abuse by an American naval officer of the good faith of a young

Japanese woman. The more likely purpose was to present a case that was representative of a practice existing in Japanese treaty ports, to shake the conscience of American readers and to raise sympathy for the victims in a kind of moral retrospect at a time that the "unequal treaties" were about to be abolished. This moral message, if not particularly profound, would still be read with approval by the sort of American public that had a subscription to the *Century Magazine*. The few new elements that Long added to the story serve the same purpose: the friendly vice-consul Sharpless's moral indignation about Pinkerton's misleading behavior and his own helpful efforts to find solutions for Butterfly's predicament; Yamadori's insistence in soliciting Butterfly's favors, which brings out more clearly her sincere loyalty to Pinkerton; Adelaide's arrival on the scene, which emphasizes Pinkerton's cowardice; and the suicide attempt, which highlights Butterfly's solitude between two cultures and two religions, a situation that Pinkerton deliberately led her to.

This is the essential difference between Loti's and Long's works. Loti's novel faithfully reflects the descriptive diary he kept, with some added elaboration on subjects such as the ongoing changes in Japan, but Long's story has the ambition of bringing a moral message to readers. To limit its intent to the purely factual rendering of one particular, real event in disguise would not only be unrealistic but also unjust to Long, as it would reduce the importance of his message without serving any substantive purpose.[5]

Long's story soon became very popular at a time when Japan still continued to intrigue Western, particularly American, audiences. It sold, as Jennie Correll said later, "like hot cakes." Its blatant sentimentality didn't seem to bother its readers. It was reprinted several times, and was included in Long's collection of Japanese stories published by the Century Company in 1898. The latter text shows small differences from the original edition; the story has been divided into fifteen chapters and touched up with numerous small, but sometimes meaningful, details that add to the authenticity of the story and its characters. Most striking in the later editions is the stronger emphasis on a certain degree of real or pretended sensuality in Butterfly and a near-professional approach in her contacts with men. This occurs in particular in her meeting with Yamadori, where she behaves as if she is deliberately trying to seduce him, but also, to an extent, in her exchanges with Sharpless, as if she knows no way to deal with men except on an intimate level.

## DAVID BELASCO

Long's story was soon noticed by one of America's most famous playwrights of that time, David Belasco. He was born in

San Francisco in a family of Anglo-Jewish immigrants who originally had come from Portugal, and he spent his youth in California and British Columbia. Following his family's tradition, he
turned to the theater and quickly became a successful author and
producer of numerous plays. He had a great sense of drama,
even in his personal appearance—he used to dress entirely in
black with a Roman collar. On the stage, he skillfully manipulat-
ed new techniques for producing light and sound effects that
stunned his audiences. Always in need of new ideas, Belasco
immediately understood the possibilities of Long's story and
started converting it into a theater play even before Long and he
had agreed on the terms.[6] Belasco did not change much with
regard to the characters of the story. He packed most of the contents into a one-act play with simple adaptations in the order of
events on the stage. Thus, the first part of Long's story (Pinkerton's stay in Nagasaki with Butterfly) is in the play revealed in
retrospect through various conversations. Pinkerton's role is
reduced to two short appearances toward the end of the play
when he returns to Nagasaki (announced by the shot of a naval
gun!) with his American wife Kate. In all he has no more than a
dozen lines. He pretends to have been mistaken about the feelings of "that little Jap girl." He tells Sharpless that when he left
Nagasaki the first time, he expected Butterfly to be ringing his
gold pieces "to make sure they're good." Because he feels inca-

pable of facing Butterfly at this time, he leaves some money with Sharpless to give to her.

Belasco's Butterfly is not very different from Long's heroine, maybe just a trifle jejune. The Sharpless of the play is the same friendly, sympathetic, but not very committed person as in the story, and Goro (who has no name in the play and is simply called "the *nakodo*," the go-between) again knows all the tricks of the game that will earn him his fee—for instance, he is the one who tells Kate that Butterfly has Pinkerton's child, thus hoping that the unavoidable trouble between the two women will force Pinkerton to announce a clear break with Butterfly so that he, Goro, can "marry" Butterfly to Yamadori. In reality the information conveyed to Kate makes her decide (apparently without consultation of her husband) to adopt the baby (who in the play has become a girl) and take possession of her at Butterfly's house. At the end of the play, we see Kate urging the reluctant Pinkerton to follow her into the house for that purpose. Without Goro's trick, Pinkerton would never have seen Butterfly again. Now he sees her the moment she dies, having committed suicide with her father's sword after uttering a few trivial words to her former lover.

The suicide at the end of the play is Belasco's most important modification. The other great addition is his scene of the vigil.[7] In Long's story Cho-Cho-san, the maid Suzuki, and the little boy spend several days and nights watching the harbor and Pinkerton's ship through little peepholes made in the paper shoji screen. Belasco transformed this part of the story into a dramatic scene on the open stage of about fifteen minutes, during which changing light and sound effects mark the passing of time from sunset to sunrise. Belasco considered this scene the greatest theatrical success of his lifelong efforts to thrill his public.

Belasco's play opened in New York on 5 March 1900. In June of that same year he brought it to the Duke of York Theatre in London. One evening in July, Giacomo Puccini, who was in London to supervise performances of his *Tosca,* saw the play. A few years later he told his friend Dante del Fiorentino that he had been able to follow the play easily although he didn't know a word of English. After the performance, Puccini said, he went backstage and embraced Belasco with tears in his eyes and asked him to allow the use of his *Madame Butterfly* as the subject of an opera. In his memoirs Belasco tells the same story in more dramatic language but the basic facts are the same. Puccini's love affair with *Butterfly* had begun.

*Almighty God touched me with*
*His little finger and said:*
*Write for the theater.*

GIACOMO PUCCINI

# 4

## The Making of an Opera

THE ITALIAN COMPOSER GIACOMO PUCCINI WAS BORN IN THE
Tuscan town of Lucca on 23 December 1858 to Michele Puccini and his wife Albina Magi. Michele, a composer and music
teacher, died in 1864 when Giacomo was only five years old. The
boy grew up in a household dominated by women, especially his
mother, to whom he was very attached and who was very close to
him. When she died in 1884, she gave him her wedding ring. His

five sisters used to hover over their brother. The only other male in the family was Giacomo's younger brother Michele, born after their father died, who as a young man went to South America, where he died at the age of twenty-seven. Puccini obtained his early musical training at the local music school of Lucca, where he learned to play the organ and the piano. He started composing when he was about sixteen years old. In 1880 he went to the Milan conservatory and received lessons in composition from Antonio Bazzini (a friend of Saint-Saëns, as previously noted) and Amilcare Ponchielli, Bazzini's successor at the conservatory. In Milan he was friendly with Pietro Mascagni and shared lodgings with him for a while. He also became acquainted with Alfredo Catalani, also from Lucca. In later life, relations with both Mascagni and Catalani were affected by jealousy because, after Giuseppe Verdi's death, Puccini gradually became Italy's most venerated musician.

In 1884 Puccini finished his first opera, *Le Villi*, and five years later his second, *Elgar*. During that period, he divided his time largely between Milan and Lucca but in 1891 he bought property in Torre del Lago, a minuscule village on the Massaciuccoli lake, which for the next thirty years would be his main home. In the following years, he composed *Manon Lescaut* (1893), *La Bohème* (1896), and *Tosca* (1900).

# On *Madama Butterfly*

The period during which Puccini worked on the initial version of *Madama Butterfly* (roughly 1901–1904) was a stormy one in his personal life. He was living in Torre del Lago with Elvira Bonturi Gemigniani, whom he had met in 1884, the year his mother died. Elvira was married at the time, a situation that would last until her husband's death in 1903, divorce not being possible in Italy at that time. Puccini and Elvira eloped in 1886 and had a son, Antonio, that same year. When Elvira's first husband finally died, Puccini, pressed by his sisters, agreed to marry Elvira in a simple ceremony in the church of Torre del Lago on 3 January 1904.

Their relationship was not in every way a happy one. Elvira, a forceful woman resembling (both physically and in character) Puccini's mother, nurtured a constant and well-founded suspicion about Puccini's affairs with other women. She tried to control his life and reproached him every time she found proof of his infidelities, which he often did not hide very successfully. There was a particularly serious crisis from approximately 1900 until 1903, when Puccini had a relationship with a certain Corinna, in correspondence often referred to as "the Piemontese" (that is, the woman of Piemont), a law student from Torino whom he had met on a train. Practically nothing else is known about her. The situation was not exceptional for Puccini, who was an accomplished womanizer, but this particular liaison lasted longer and seemed to be more serious than usual. Toward its end, the affair became atrocious as lawyers were brought in to handle the breakup and financial settlement. The case worried Puccini's publisher Giulio Ricordi and other friends, and, of course, his sisters. A number of individual and concerted actions were required to convince Puccini that he should end the affair. A serious car accident that, early in 1903, immobilized him for several months contributed to a final break with Corinna later that year. His subsequent marriage with Elvira seems to have been agreed upon by Puccini partly out of loyalty to his companion of nearly eighteen years but also partly to present Corinna with a fait accompli that hopefully would stop any attempts to blackmail him into a marriage with her. Both the affair and the relationship with Elvira must have been very much on Puccini's mind during the years he was composing *Madama Butterfly.*

For the making of this opera, Puccini selected a team consisting of Giuseppe Giacosa and Luigi Illica as librettists and his publisher, Giulio Ricordi. Giacosa and Illica had already worked jointly with Puccini on *La Bohème* and *Tosca.* They were used to a distribution of labor between them in which Illica first drafted the dramatic structure and the dialogues and Giacosa subsequently turned these into verse. Both men had, besides qualities in their own fields, personal experiences that could be useful in their work on *Madama Butterfly*: Giacosa was an enthusiastic reader of Japanese poetry, and Illica was the librettist of Mascagni's opera *Iris*. Ricordi was the fatherly friend of all, ready to help in solving problems or incompatibilities whenever they arose. There were enough of those not only because the composer and the librettists were strong-minded characters, each of them firmly believing in his own artistic ideas, but also because their work was from the beginning based on two partly overlapping but still different sources: Long's story and Belasco's play (hereafter "the novel" and "the play"). There was no agreement between them concerning the order of priority between these sources. Under such circumstances, existing differences in the appreciation of literary, musical, and, eventually, commercial requirements naturally were blown up out of all proportion by the powerful egos of the members of the team. In following as closely as possible the chronological order of events in the genesis of *Madama Butterfly*, I shall try to clarify some of the enigmas surrounding the opera and give answers to a few of the questions that are often raised.

THE GENESIS

Upon his return to Torre del Lago from London, where he had seen Belasco's play in the summer of 1900, Puccini began

*Giacomo Puccini in 1913.*

his attempts to obtain from the author the rights to use the *Madame Butterfly* story, duly assisted by Ricordi and by Ricordi's agent in the United States. Meanwhile, he pursued other ideas for a new opera but his mind returned more and more often to Belasco's little drama that had made such a deep impression on him. Puccini was already aware at that time of the existence of the novel: in a letter to Ricordi of 20 November 1900, he suggests that Illica will find in the novel the necessary material to use but he also expresses a clear preference for the play, which he thought could be the basis for the second act (with the first act taking place in North America). This initial idea of an American act was, however, soon abandoned as having no relevance to the subject.

On 7 March 1901, Puccini sent Illica the Italian translation of the novel and emphasized his continued interest in the play and his endorsement of the changes Belasco made vis-à-vis the novel. When Illica showed a positive reaction to the idea of an opera on this subject, Puccini urged him to convey this feeling to Ricordi, who had remained hesitant about it even after Puccini read the novel to him. Illica complied with his suggestion and told Ricordi about his enthusiasm, adding that he was already working on the first act and that the finale of that act would be even better than the end of the first act of *La Bohème*. By this time the agreed schedule included three acts, all set in Japan, of which two would be located in Butterfly's house in Nagasaki (one of these taken from Long's novel and the other one from Belasco's play) and the third would take place in the American consulate in that city (also taken from Long).[1]

In April 1901, Puccini reported to Illica that he had acquired the rights to the play.[2] Illica, who had thus far been working on his draft on the basis of the novel (he even received another Italian translation from Puccini, who was afraid that the first one was not correct), reacted to that news in a letter to Ricordi of the same month by saying that there was no need to obtain Belasco's permission or to pay him for it because the last act could basically be found in Long's novel. Illica thought that Puccini overrated the dramatic effects of Belasco's scenic details (which, incidentally, Illica could not know firsthand as he had not seen the play and would not have an Italian translation of it until June) and felt that he and Giacosa would be able to make something better than the play. His strong preference for the novel over the play could have been motivated by contempt for Belasco's poor literary talent and tendency to stage for sensational effect. But Illica was correct in believing that Long's novel gives a more profound image of the differences between the American sailor and the Japanese woman.[3]

As for Puccini, he clearly preferred the play, perhaps because he had a strong recollection of its theatrical effects. Belasco's remark that Puccini had not really seen his play but had just heard the music he would write is a little inaccurate but it touches upon a well-known aspect of the composer's personality. Puccini's biographers are unanimous in describing him as a man of an emotional rather than rational attitude, with sometimes imprecise but always very intense feelings and little ability for profound analysis. This state of mind explains his preference for the theater over reading and his natural inclination to approach his dramas in a very visual way.[4] When in 1900 Puccini was considering an opera based on Alphonse Daudet's *Tartarin de Tarascon*, he described the finale in a letter to Illica entirely in terms of scenery, light, and colors, without a word about the music.[5] A few year later, in 1907, he did the same thing to describe his feelings about "La Fianciulla del West" as the subject for an opera: it's all forest, trees, and horses but no notes.[6]

One recognizes the same phenomenon in Puccini's work on *Madama Butterfly:* he wrote often about the details of stage direct-

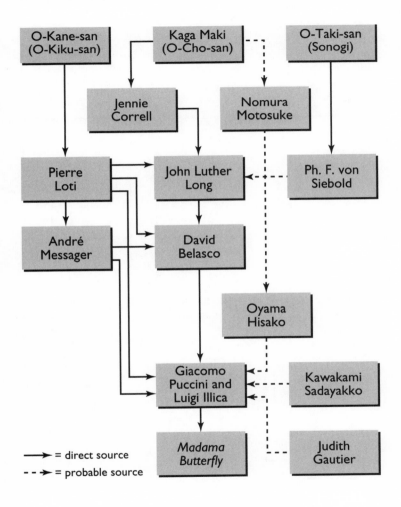

*Dramatic Genealogy* of Madama Butterfly.

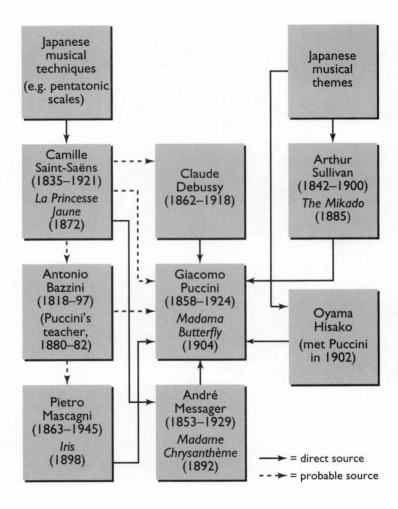

*Sources for some of Puccini's Japanese Music.*

ing and was very impressed by such magical effects as the vigil.
When eventually he turns his visual impressions into music, one
can easily discern the emotion he felt at several points during the
play. Most notably, the scene of the vigil comes to life in the
intermezzo at the end of act 2.[7] There are many other examples
of Puccini's emotional and very visual understanding of the play:
Yamadori's pompous entrance, Butterfly's surprise to see Sharpless enter her house, Suzuki's shock to find Pinkerton and Sharpless knocking at the door at the end of the last act, and the shot
of the naval gun when Pinkerton's ship returns—these are all
moments of theatrical delight that Puccini remembered when he
turned the story into music. He obviously enjoyed the play thor-
oughly and in spite of the language barrier understood it. That
was one reason why he insisted on a better use of the play. He
even invited Illica to come with him to London and see it for
himself (but they did not do this). Illica initially continued
working with the novel and accumulating from it, as he put it,
"even too many opportunities" to be put to music, while agree-
ing that a selection would be necessary later on. And in order not
to upset his team at this time, Puccini confirmed in a letter to
Giacosa of 20 May 1901, that he considered the "prologue"
that he had received from Illica to be most successful.[8]

Early in June of 1901, Puccini finally managed to get an Italian text of the play. He read it to Ricordi, who gradually over-

came his initial hesitation and began to agree that they were heading for another success. A copy was sent to Illica, who had finished his first draft of act I but had yet to start on the second. This became more urgent now; Illica's contributions were to be turned into verse by Giacosa before Puccini could start working on the music. The composer began to be nervous and at times desperate because of the delay. He sent letter upon letter to Ricordi, Illica, and Giacosa, complaining about the long time it took to produce something that he could work on. Reproaches went in particular to Giacosa. In October Puccini received Illica's drafts of two more acts, but only in November did he get Giacosa's work on act I—and without the final love scene.[9]

## THE EARLY DRAFT

Finished in May 1901, Illica's draft of act I is his earliest known contribution and the only early draft that survived in its original (handwritten) form. This draft contains all the elements of the present act I but also many more and with much more elaborated detail. It displays a mood different from that of the final libretto. Based on the first pages of Long's novel (admittedly not enough for an entire act of an opera), it adopted numerous ideas from elsewhere. For example, Illica introduced some elements that seem to come from Messager's *Madame Chrysanthème*, such as the arrival of Butterfly's family and Goro's introduction of the family. But many scenes come from Loti and, curiously, many of these are presented with the "comical" note that is one of the hallmarks of Loti's style.[10] In this draft, one is struck by the crude way Illica presents Pinkerton's jokes about (and contempt for) the Japanese. While both the amusement and the disdain are very present in Loti's novel, there they are mixed with a degree of tenderness and sympathy for a Japanese culture bound to be destroyed (in Loti's eyes) by Western modernism. None of that is in Illica's draft. A few Americanisms, which one does not find in Long nor, obviously, in Loti, appear to be Illica's original contributions; they were woven into the story much to the delight of Puccini, who took great pleasure in emphasizing the contrast between Eastern and Western attitudes. (For example, Pinkerton should sing in an "American way" but the Japanese women should move and speak as they did in real-life in Japan.)[11]

One gets the impression that in his eagerness to show these contrasts, Illica went a little too far and had to be corrected later on. It was not the only mistake. Butterfly is called a "geisha," an erroneous title that neither Loti nor Long used (Belasco did use this word, but as noted earlier Illica didn't want to borrow from him). His decision to introduce Pinkerton as a Britisher under

the name of Sir Francis Blummy Pinkerton is difficult to understand as it lacks any logical connection with the story; the odd
title and the name were eventually removed but only after the
premiere of the opera at La Scala in 1904 (and the initials F. B.
had a long life into most modern versions of the libretto).
Equally unclear in this first draft is why Illica associates Sharpless so closely with Pinkerton's crude humor, while describing
him in a letter to Ricordi of early 1901 as "a bluff, jovial man,
good, at heart philosophical and, after living in various countries,
scornful of all fads and customs, appreciating now only good
people, whether they be English or Boers or Japanese."[12] Perhaps
Illica's description of Pinkerton as a colonial barbarian and ugly
American was simply his way of staying with Long's novel and
avoiding using Belasco's play.

    As Illica had already foreseen, much of his initial draft had to
be eliminated. When compared to Puccini's autograph score of
the completed opera and the printed piano-vocal score used at
the 17 February 1904 premiere, which are nearly identical docu-
ments, it becomes clear that between 1901 and 1904 about
one-half of Illica's first draft of act I disappeared and the rest
underwent numerous changes. For most of these differences, one
can only guess who requested what and why, but it is striking to
see that most of the "comical" and crude elements and a number
of superfluous or too elaborate scenes were cut or drastically

shortened. The result was a better balanced first act with more focus on the characters but still emphasizing tensions between East and West.

## MORE CHANGES

By autumn of 1901, Puccini had a total of three drafts from Illica: act 1, which he had received in May, and act 2 (at Butterfly's house) and act 3 (the consulate scene), which he received in October. In November he received Giacosa's (still incomplete) version of act 1, which enabled him to finally do systematic work on the composition. From there on, the letters between members of the team show a nearly endless exchange of ideas and suggestions for changes, initiated by Puccini and often driving the others to despair. Giacosa complained regularly about the impossibility of making progress on later parts of the opera if Puccini constantly required changes in earlier parts. But in spite of such altercations, the work advanced at a moderate pace.

To give his opera an exotic flavor and in keeping with the practices of Japonisme, Puccini was eagerly looking for original Japanese material. In April 1902, he met Kawakami Sadayakko in Milan, where her husband Otojiro was producing his plays, to get an impression of the manner in which Japanese women speak and use body language. He reviewed Japanese musical themes, some

*Oyama Hisako, the wife of Oyama Tsunasuke, Japan's minister to Rome from about 1900 to 1906. (Courtesy Professor Sawada Toshio)*

of which he might have found in Messager's *Madame Chrysanthème*. He could have been acquainted with the use of pentatonic scales by his teacher Bazzini, who in earlier days had witnessed Saint-Saëns use this technique for the first time in Europe. The pentatonic scale used in act 2 for the arrival of Prince Yamadori (which actually is the tune of the Japanese army war song "Miya sama") most likely came from act 2 of *The Mikado*. The sword motif and the sailors' chorus were taken from Debussy's *Pelléas*. Puccini also consulted Mrs. Oyama Hisako, the wife of the Japanese minister in Rome. In September and October 1902, they met several times; she sang Japanese melodies for him, supplied him with phonograph records of Japanese music, and promised to find him scores of more melodies. She enhanced his pleasure in his subject by telling him that she knew a real-life story exactly like that of Butterfly's. She criticized some of the names he used and Puccini followed her advice, except on Prince Yamadori.

Mrs. Oyama was the main source of most of the seven authentically Japanese themes used by Puccini that Mosco Carner identified in his biography of the composer. In adopting original Japanese music, using Japanese techniques such as the pentatonic scale, and creating quasi-Japanese effects produced by classical European musical techniques and instruments, Puccini not only made *Madama Butterfly* into a work in true Japonisme style but he displayed even more fondness of Japonisme in music than any other European composer.

Shortly after his sessions with Mrs. Oyama, Puccini suddenly decided on a very dramatic change in the concept of the opera. In several letters dated 16 November 1902, he admits to his team that the consulate scene (act 3) has been a serious mistake and that he is now convinced that the opera must be reduced to two acts to keep up with the development of an effective and frightening drama.

Although unhappy with this unexpected change, Puccini's team complied with his wish to enhance the dynamism of the opera that from now on would have two parts: one based on Illica's first draft (inspired by the novel) and another that followed the play. Both Illica and Giacosa argued that the second act (now amplified with what necessarily had to be carried over from the eliminated consulate scene) would be too long and should be cut into two separate acts. In particular Giacosa warned that main-

taining one long second act would cause a disaster with the public, but Puccini refused to give in.

What could have caused this sudden change? What did Puccini have in mind when in his letters to Ricordi of November
1902 he speaks of a "dilution" of his work by the consulate act
and argues that, instead, the action should move forward "without interruption, rapid, effective, terrible"? It is hard to guess
what exactly irked him because we do not know what was in that
act—no text has survived. Most likely its contents were close to
the part of Long's novel where Butterfly comes to the consulate
for the second time and discovers that Pinkerton is married in
America and that his wife wants to take Butterfly's child, a scene
that does not exist in the play. In Long's scene, the direct
exchange between Butterfly and Mrs. Pinkerton is limited to a
few lines that have little to do with the main issues; the drama is
entirely in the accidental discovery of the real facts. There is an
element of East-West confrontation in that part of the novel but
it is between Butterfly and the consul. From that point of view,
the act would have been a little superfluous after the abundant
East-versus-West situations of the first act. Puccini's decision
must be seen as a deliberate and forceful return to the end of
Belasco's play with the much more substantive and painful
exchange at Butterfly's house between the two women about such
matters as Pinkerton's marriage and Butterfly's child and includ-

ing the offensive offer by Pinkerton of money as a compensation for Butterfly's sacrifice. The new ending of the opera is more a crude confrontation between two women with different characters and interests than it is an East-West contrast. Puccini's personal situation at that time was so close to this scene that it is impossible not to suppose that it influenced his decision. The nearing end of his relationship with Corinna, the pressure of his friends to sever his ties with her, Elvira's shrewd stratagems to pursue the outcome she wished, and the threat of negotiations for a financial settlement are reflected in the new conclusion of Butterfly's drama.[13]

## Puccini's Psychological Underpinnings

Puccini's apparently largely unconscious attitudes toward women in general and the heroines of his operas in particular are a fascinating topic of study. Anybody who has seen Puccini's last opera, *Turandot*, the conclusion of which features the hero, Calaf, embracing the icy princess after having attended passively the torture and suicide of the lovable slave girl Li, must wonder, as I do, why no psychoanalytical biography of Puccini has been written yet. Few cases in history of early neurosis appear to be so rich in substance and in consequences for the work of a creative artist as that of Puccini. Extensive research might shed light on this facet of much of his work. Of all of Puccini's biographers, the only one who examines this subject in some detail is Mosco Carner, in his critical 1958 biography. Carner postulates that Puccini's strong, unconscious mother fixation was and remained throughout most of his life a main driving force behind his social behavior and his artistic activity.

Carner's argument is that Puccini's bondage to his mother, a strong-willed person who loved and cherished her son and sacrificed much to make him succeed in his musical studies, explains both his tendency to avoid lasting relationships with superior women other than his wife Elvira as well as his multiple escapes into small adventures with easy and submissive women. According to Carner, Puccini projected onto these passive partners the feeling of dominance that he could not display toward Elvira, the powerful wife/mother, and that he needed to display to offset his dependency on her. The quasi-incest that in Puccini's mind was associated with these sexual adventures (because of the substitution of other women for the dominating mother) would lead to feelings of guilt and an unconscious need to denigrate the "unworthy" women; they should be placed at a lower level than the mother to make the temporary relationship possible at all. This, according to Carner, is transposed into Puccini's operas. Most of his heroines are socially inferior in one way or the other: Mimi of *La Bohème*, Manon of *Manon Lescaut, Tosca, But-*

*terfly,* Magda of *La Rondine,* Giorgetta of *Il Tabarro,* and Angelica of *Suor Angelica* all have or have had at one time a questionable morality in their relations with men. The slave girl Li of *Turandot* and the barmaid Minnie of *La Fanciulla del West* belong in other ways to socially inferior categories. Puccini not only shows a compulsive preference for such heroines but he lets his feelings about them run freely to the point of making them into "shining little angels," as Carner calls them. On the other hand, the forbidden desire has to be repressed and the women punished, because his heroines are rivals to the mother and compete with her for his love. Thus, nearly all Puccini's heroines are killed, commit suicide, die miserably, or are punished in some other way, particularly by the forced return to a life that they do not want. Butterfly clearly belongs to this category of "unworthy" women: she sells herself for a hundred yen to a foreign sailor whom initially she considers to be a "barbarian" American. But she is also honest and principled and her love for Pinkerton (which is spontaneous and comes at an early moment, as Sharpless tells Pinkerton) leads her to a pure and loyal (albeit erroneous) commitment. In the end, however, she will have to step back behind his "real" spouse. Between two kinds of punishment—return to a life of professionally entertaining men or die—she opts for the second because she cannot live any longer with honor.

Carner also argues that Puccini could only begin to have a more balanced view of women and deal with real love as a "benign force" when, around sixty years old, he finally became a more mature man, albeit hesitantly even then. He finally allowed the "mother" image to appear in his later operas—for example, the aunt in *Suor Angelica* and the princess in *Turandot*—but only in *Turandot* did he make an attempt (and not even very successfully, argues Carner) to transform the cruel princess into a loving wife. Carner does not address *Madama Butterfly* in this context, although it seems to me that Puccini already tried in a much earlier stage of his life (coinciding with his marriage with Elvira) to face the cruel mother/wife in the person of Kate Pinkerton, who shows much resemblance with the cold and arrogant personality of the aunt in *Suor Angelica*. The libretto of the earliest version of the opera (performed in Milan in 1904) confronts us with a selfish and calculating Kate, interfering in a cold way with her husband's past business, trying to solve the ensuing problems in a way that fits her interests, and who, in the process, wants to be forgiven for it by her victim. There is not much love in Kate even if the stage directions require her to be "deeply moved."

If one accepts that Puccini lived with such neurotic fixations (which I think is obvious), it becomes much easier to understand the decisions he made regarding the shape of the opera's ending in its earliest version, which compress and strengthen the drama of his heroine and return to Belasco's view of the confrontation between the two women that had moved him so much when he saw it for the first time on the stage of the Duke of York Theatre.

In the case of a personality like Puccini's, one is inclined to search for other personal factors that could have influenced the direction of his artistic decisions. Could, for instance, Puccini have been influenced also by feelings awakened by Mrs. Oyama? They met for the first time just before his affair with Corinna turned sour. Mrs. Oyama flattered the composer with her interest in his work and his subject at a moment when he felt abandoned by his family and his friends and badly in need of such sympathy. Puccini's letters to Ricordi of the autumn of 1902 describe her as intelligent and attractive and refer to a number of sessions they had during which she talked about Japan and sang Japanese songs. His interest in her appears to be more than superficial. If it is true that Puccini, easily moved by attractive women, saw Butterfly as "Hisako Oyama in disguise," there would be an additional motive for him to concentrate more strongly on her personality and let her shine more before the end comes.[14]

## Completion of the Opera

Early in January 1903 there was another exchange of violent letters. Giacosa pleaded that Puccini, for the sake of a better balance of the opera, not resist any longer the splitting of the last
act into two separate ones; he admitted that this would be a
departure from the play but since it had already been agreed that
the play could not be the exclusive origin of material (because
the first act was based on the novel), there was no good reason
not to go further and split act 2. But Puccini refused and Giacosa gave in. Later events would show that this was a major mistake and that Giacosa had been right.

On 25 February 1903, Puccini had a serious car accident that
left him temporarily crippled and unable to work until June.
That month Ricordi and Giacosa came to visit him and gave him
the now finally completed draft libretto of the entire opera in
two acts. Puccini remained slightly handicapped and often very
depressed, but in August he suddenly seemed to feel in high spirits again and reported to Ricordi that he was working on the
orchestration of the second act of the "little Japanese miss."
After that the work proceeded smoothly and the orchestration of
the opera was completed on 27 December 1903, at 11:10 P.M.

There was a short personal interlude. Elvira's husband died
on 26 February 1903 (a few hours after Puccini's accident!), and

this development allowed Puccini and Elvira to legitimize their relationship. Efforts were made, and energetically pushed by Puccini's sisters, to request a dispensation of the rule of Italian law that a widow cannot remarry within ten months of her husband's death, but those efforts were given up eventually. The wedding took place on 3 January 1904, in Torre del Lago. How reluctant Puccini felt about this union can be surmised from the letter he sent to his sister Ramelde the day after, where he asks her, "Are you happy now?" and, more crudely, from a cartoon he sent to his friends to announce the marriage in which he stands nearly naked next to a dressed Elvira.

A last dramatic protest came from Giacosa early in January 1904 shortly before the premiere of *Madama Butterfly* in Milan. He addressed it to Ricordi, who had informed him of Puccini's decision to eliminate some of Giacosa's lines for Pinkerton at the end of the last act. Giacosa furiously refused to agree and emphasized the need to maintain an aria for the tenor at that place. Ridiculous solutions were discussed, such as maintaining the text in the printed libretto in brackets but not actually singing it. Giacosa protested the "butchering" of his work but eventually gave in as he had done before. And, again, history would show that he had been right.

## DISASTER IN MILAN

The premiere of *Madama Butterfly*, which Puccini at the last moment had dedicated to Queen Elena of Italy, took place on 17 February 1904, at the Teatro alla Scala in Milan. This performance remains one of the most famous disasters of modern musical history. The opera was received with laughter and hostility caused, it seems, by a combination of intrinsic weaknesses of the work (particularly the length of the second act and a very untraditional role for the leading tenor) and the well-organized action of a strong anti-Puccini mob. Although Puccini was not certain about how much of the riot was spontaneous and how much was orchestrated, he felt forced by the turmoil in the Scala to reconsider some of his earlier decisions on the balance and duration of the opera. He also felt strongly enough about the quality of his work that he maintained most of what he had written. In a letter to his friend Camillo Bondi of 22 February 1904, he is clear that he will rewrite only a few details, make a few cuts, and divide act 2. And so, belatedly, he gave in to Giacosa: act 2 was split into part 1 and part 2; Sharpless and Pinkerton were given a few more lines at the end of the last act; and Pinkerton got a short aria at the end ("Addio, fiorito asil"), the same one that in January had been cut against Giacosa's protest. Puccini also gave Butterfly a new emotional outburst after she has spotted Pinkerton's ship upon its return ("Trionfa il mio amor"). A scene in the first act where Butterfly's uncle Yakuside sings, drinks, and gibbers some incoherent if not vulgar Japanese rhymes was eliminated along with a few smaller cuts.

## SUCCESS AT LAST

In this revised form, the opera was performed again in the Teatro Grande in Brescia on 28 May 1904. This time it was a great success and a triumph for Puccini. But he did not leave the opera in this shape. In the following years, it was performed in Buenos Aires, London, Bologna, and Budapest with additional changes (particularly after the London performance of 1905). Then, in preparation for the production in the Opéra Comique in Paris on 28 December 1906, more important alterations were made at the initiative of Albert Carré, director of the Opéra Comique and husband of Marguérite Carré, who was to sing the title role. Carré wanted to accommodate his French public and perhaps adapt Butterfly's role to his wife's personality. Giulio Ricordi disagreed with Carré on several adaptations but his son Tito, who represented him on this occasion, was already thinking of the North American tour of the opera organized for 1907. Some changes proposed by Carré would have the advantage of making the opera look better in the eyes of the American public, with obvious commercial consequences. Tito Ricordi convinced Puccini upon his arrival in Paris late in 1906 to go along with many of Carré's suggestions.

One of the most striking changes in the Parisian version (besides the decision to change the two parts of act 2 into act 2 and act 3) is the replacement of the words (but not the music!) of a part of Butterfly's aria "Che tua madre" in act 2, just before Sharpless leaves: after imagining that she might have to return to her earlier ways of earning a living by dancing and singing, the initial text included Butterfly's fantasy about meeting the emperor of Japan, who might make her son Dolore a prince (an idea that came from Long's novel); in the new libretto she rejects the idea of returning to her old way of life, saying that she would rather die. Many critics believe that this self-pitying version is a poor substitution for the dignified dream about the emperor. What strikes me, however, is that the music of the aria has not been changed and that the new words actually go better with the music. As for the rest of Carré's wishes: a few lines that cast a negative image of Pinkerton were cut (for example, where Butterfly refers to him as "barbarian") as well as Butterfly's confession that she was paid a hundred yen for her services. At the very end, some of Kate's lines were given to Sharpless, changed, or cut to soften the impression she makes. As a result, Butterfly's personality dominates the final scene of the opera more than before, the American couple looks less offensive, and the final scene is less crude. Kate's part has been drastically reduced.

In addition to scenic improvements invented by Carré (an aspect for which Puccini always had a great sensitivity) it must have been the strengthening of Butterfly's personality in the final scene that Tito Ricordi used to convince Puccini to accept changes that, prior to his departure for Paris, he had seemed resolved to refuse. Soon after his arrival in Paris, however, he largely endorsed Carré's alterations. In a letter to Giulio Ricordi in November he defended them enthusiastically for reasons that have only to do with the mise-en-scène and said he was pleased with the fact that Kate lost most of her part and is now left out in the garden. He fully accepted that the dramatic tension between Kate and Butterfly, which he had deliberately introduced in the Milan version and maintained since, was reduced in favor of a more shining role for Butterfly. It is as if he was not yet certain about what the character of Kate meant to him.

This version of the opera has become the standard. Whether one prefers earlier variants or not, it is a fact that in the Parisian version Butterfly takes the dramatic dimension—the dignity, humanity, loyalty, and strength—that the opera public has become accustomed to and that it loves so much. In spite of some differences, Puccini's heroine ultimately is closest to Long's in the clarity of her understanding of the contract that links her to Pinkerton, her true feelings of love for him that come at a very early moment and that she tells him are *"per la vita"* (for life), and the reasons she sees for assuming that he wants to remain married to her. As in Long's novel, she has a certain playfulness in dealing with difficult situations (such as Yamadori's efforts to seduce her) and a lively mind, ready to give a quick, sarcastic reply to the cousin who pretends to have rejected Pinkerton's proposal before her. In a more serious vein, and again as in Long's novel, she flirts with the idea of a conversion to Christianity, and it is only in the end that her kneeling before the Buddha statue indicates her return to a Japanese faith. Finally, Belasco's solution of a suicide determines the course of events, leaving intact Butterfly's dignity and integrity.

In Pinkerton's case, there were various models in the sources that had been used: an interested but uncommitted French officer and writer, seen by himself; a superficial, hedonistic American officer seen by an American writer with a strong moralistic bias; and, finally, a near nonentity in Belasco's play. Illica, who despised the play, used the other two sources, and with the artistic license of a European author writing about an American officer, he mixed both models: his Pinkerton is definitely Long's officer but with a number of Loti's sarcastic attitudes. Initially, Illica made him more cynical than his models but gradually the character was softened; eventually, he was even given some sym-

pathetic touches mostly because it was felt that the public wanted a more traditional type of tenor.

As for the other characters: Pinkerton's arrogant wife Kate
(who initially was clearly the stronger person in the couple, an
idea that came from the play) was in the final version reduced to
almost nothing. Sharpless (a vice-consul in Long's story, he is
since Belasco's play promoted to consul) remains the weak but
sympathetic advocate of humane behavior that is depicted in the
novel, and incorporates the helpful attitudes of Loti's friend Yves
and their "very tall friend." Suzuki is the straightforward and
loyal friend. Goro, the selfish but explicit go-between, also
remains true to Long's novel. Yamadori is a less ridiculous frus-
trated lover than in Belasco's treatment, and there is clear sympathy with him expressed in the music at the moments of his
arrival and exit as if Puccini identified with his feelings. After all,
he would prefer to hide behind Yamadori rather than be identified with Pinkerton.

If the Parisian version of the score received the official bless-
ing of Puccini and Giulio Ricordi, there is still another, slightly
adapted version, that was performed in the Teatro Carcano in
Milan after World War I and in which, according to the conductor Tenaglia, some phrases that had been deleted were reinserted
with the authorization of Puccini: the description of Butterfly's
two uncles (the bonze and the drunk), Uncle Yakuside's drinking

bout, and the lines in the love duet where Butterfly admits or reveals her initial fear of marrying a "barbarian" American. If indeed Puccini agreed on these small changes, it shows that toward the end of his life he was ready to return to some of the elements that came from Long's novel. His librettists would have been grateful for that sign of recognition but they were not there any longer: Giacosa died in 1906 and Illica in 1919.

*History is merely gossip.*

OSCAR WILDE

# 5

## Real-Life Models

ONE OF THE EXTRAORDINARY ASPECTS OF THE *BUTTERFLY* STORY is the presence of a real-life story underneath. As discussed in Chapter 3, the immediate source of John Luther Long's novel is the story his sister told him in 1897 in Philadelphia. Even if we have only a few very short versions of it, all revealed at least thirty-four years after the facts, our curiosity is still tickled by the real events. Attempts have been made by some authors, some serious and some not so serious, to penetrate the secrets behind Jennie Correll's story but none of them has been very conclusive.[1]

One thing should be kept in mind from the outset: much of the material of Long's novel comes straight from Loti, which in one sense leaves little mystery around the characters taken from that source because they are in most cases openly referred to in Loti's diary, often with their real names. But those characters were just borrowed to give Long's story a more elaborate structure; they do not lift the veil that hangs over the identity of the persons Mrs. Correll talked about. Her story (in particular, the version in the *Japan Magazine*) mentions only two main roles in the drama: Cho-san and her lover, whose name, nationality, and profession are not mentioned. In Long's novel, Pinkerton is largely inspired by Loti's lieutenant, whereas Madame Butterfly, the main character, is entirely modeled by Long himself—but both are based on real persons. To find their real-life models, we have to use the only key we have: Mrs. Correll's story.

## How Reliable Is Jennie Correll?

One important problem here is that our principal witness, Jennie Correll, is not a very reliable one. Certainly, it was she who originally heard the story in Nagasaki and passed it on to her brother when she returned to Philadelphia in 1897. We can assume that, as a solid nineteenth-century Methodist American missionary's wife, she would not just have made it up and then persisted in telling the lie. Besides, this was a normally occurring event in the Nagasaki treaty port and Mrs. Oyama also told Puccini that she knew the story, or at least something closely resembling it. But Jennie Correll, who had her own idealistic (and respectable) motives to carry the story to the American public, would, at least initially, focus more on the message than on the facts. Relating the real facts too explicitly (presuming she knew them all with certainty) could only bring her embarrassment at that time. When finally, in 1931, she publicly addressed the facts, she didn't give the impression of being free of sensationalism. In the record of her talk on 13 March 1931, revised by herself and published in the *Japan Magazine,* Jennie emphasized the "secret" about the origin of the story that was known, she said, "only to two persons of whom I am one and it is now for the first time revealed."[2] This slightly inflated language indicates the simple fact that she and her brother were the only ones who knew the original story (omitting in the process, I presume, her own husband, whom she normally would have informed). We know that John Luther Long was familiar with the real story because (as we will see) he told it to the soprano Miura Tamaki—but back in 1898 his pride of authorship had not included the disclosure of

his sources and in the introduction to the 1903 edition of the
novel he just gave a few hints of what he knew about Butterfly
and Pinkerton. Irvin Correll died in 1926 and John Luther Long
died in 1927. Apparently Jennie then felt that the time had come
to tell the world that it was she who had heard the original story
for the first time and she did it with such a degree of melodra-
matic pontification that one can only wonder if it was not the
thrill of the conspiracy that guided her rather than the need to
explore the real events. Strictly speaking there was no such need
at all, since the success of the story had already satisfied her initial motives for giving it such wide publicity; it was now a short
story, a play, and an opera. Also, how good was Jennie's memory
in her eighty-second year of life about facts that she had heard
over thirty years earlier?

Jennie Correll's versions of her story show the inaccuracies
and contradictions that come with such a long time span. For
example, the English version of the *Japan Magazine* article suggests
the personal acquaintance of a group of people, to which Jennie
belongs, with the teahouse girl Cho-san ("Everyone was in love
with her. In time we learned that she had a lover . . .") but then
turns the denouement of the abandonment into a fact reported
by others ("There was quite a sensation when it was learned . . ."). 
Also, the story presents as a sudden, recent event ("One evening
there was quite a sensation . . ." ) a situation that necessarily must

have developed and degenerated slowly (the long waiting for the lover's return and the gradual understanding that he will not come back), which, again, suggests the reporting by an outsider after the moment that the nonreturn has become evident. The same article also mentions the presence of a baby but does not specify whether it was born before or after the father's departure, a detail that a woman in Jennie's position would normally pay attention to if she knew the case personally. The Japanese *Jiji Shimpo* article also contains the first of these contradictions ("I became involved . . ." versus "From my usual shopkeeper I heard . . .") and it also brings up the issue of Cho-san's death, which is omitted in both English versions. In none of the three versions is there any reference to the lover's nationality or profession or his eventual return.

## So What Are the Facts?

All these facts give us the clear impression that Jennie was not really involved herself in the story at all but that she just heard it from others. Therefore, we should try to deduce from the story, as told, the location and the time of the event. The place is simple: the story occurred in Nagasaki, and we even know the detail that Cho-san lived "on the hill opposite ours." There are many hills in Nagasaki and some of them can be considered to be opposite of Higashi Yamate, where the Corrells lived. The most obvious one, Minami Yamate, must be excluded because this hill belonged to the foreign concession and it would be unthinkable that a Japanese teahouse girl, living alone since the departure of her lover, would reside inside the concession, particularly in this prestigious, slightly snobbish, and overwhelmingly European part of it. Neither the foreigners nor the Japanese authorities would have tolerated such a thing.[3] There is, however, another "opposite hill" nearby, Kojimamachi, a neighborhood located outside the concession where some foreigners had houses that they could rent or hold under Japanese law on the basis of a right of superficies for 999 years. Some foreigners had a secondary residence in Kojimamachi for the purpose of keeping a Japanese woman.[4] The teahouse where Cho-san was likely to work while waiting for the return of her lover would normally be located in the Maruyama pleasure quarter just adjacent to the Kojimamachi hill. But there is, of course, no certainty that Jennie referred to this particular hill. There are a few others, slightly more remote, that could also be considered "opposite."

The timing of the event is more relevant but also more complicated. The Corrells were posted in Nagasaki approximately from 1892 until 1897. Irvin Correll was headmaster of Chinzei Gakkan on Higashi Yamate in 1892 and 1893 but the couple stayed in Nagasaki after that for five years before leaving for

America in 1897. In her talks of 1931 (published in *Jiji Shimpo*), Jennie Correll mentioned that the moment she became "involved" was "thirty-four years ago"—1897. In the autumn of that year she told her brother about the event. If it was recent then and she had been "involved" herself, it must have happened just before the Corrells' departure from Nagasaki. If, however, she just heard it from somebody else, it could have occurred at a much earlier time. In the latter case, we have no clue in Jennie's story for timing the event. Abandonment of pregnant Japanese women by foreign visitors was frequent enough, but there must have been a new development that brought back the memory of the earlier case at the time that Jennie Correll heard about it.

An additional problem for the timing is the absence of the lover's return in Jennie's story. The appearance and subsequent departure of Pinkerton's ship as told in Long's novel could have been the cause of "quite a sensation," but as Jennie does not mention such an event, it is not clear why Cho-san should suddenly have given up waiting. If in her despair she tried to take her life, the sudden "sensation" would have been caused by the suicide attempt (whether followed by death, as in the *Jiji Shimpo* article, or not, as later told by Long) and not by the abandonment Jennie referred to. One could very well assume that the suicide attempt was the real cause of the "sensation" but that in her

talks to an English-speaking audience in Tokyo Jennie preferred
to refrain from elaborating on an act so contrary to her Christian
beliefs. The suicide attempt not followed by death seems to be
confirmed by Japanese soprano Miura Tamaki, who in an interview of 1935 states that John Luther Long had told her that the
original Cho-san had survived it.[5] In his introduction to the
1903 edition of the story, John Luther Long does not mention
the suicide attempt but he says that Cho-san is both a "fancy"
and a living person. So if indeed there was a suicide attempt, the
woman must have survived it. If Jennie spoke before her Japanese
audience of Cho-san's death, she can only have meant her eventual death at a later date.[6]

There is evidence, however, that in reality the story as reported by Jennie was based on a much older event and that she was
only informed of it much later, when she lived in Nagasaki. A
number of authors quote Miura Tamaki as the source of a disclosure of the son of the real-life Butterfly, whom Jennie refers to
in the *Japan Magazine* version of her story. She has been quoted as
saying that Long had told her that the real name of Butterfly's
child was Tom Glover, that the child had been known to Mrs.
Correll, and that the father had not been a naval officer (as in
Long's story) but an English merchant in Nagasaki.[7]

# Tom Glover: Butterfly's Son?

Miura Tamaki's story is confirmed by none other than Tom Glover himself, whose Japanese name was Guraba Tomisaburo and who also called himself Tomisaburo Awajiya Guraba (with the Western order of first name, middle name, family name). "Awajiya" was his mother's family name, and "Guraba" the Japanese transliteration of the English "Glover." He was believed to be the natural son of the Scottish (not English) merchant Thomas B. Glover and his Japanese common-law wife Awajiya Tsuru (sometimes referred to as Yamamura Tsuru, after her first husband). In a book about Tsuru's life, the author Noda Heinosuke tells how he became acquainted with the administrative employee of the British consulate in Nagasaki, Ikegami Heizo, who described to him a meeting that took place in 1931 or 1932, in his presence, between Guraba Tomi-

*Thomas Glover in his mid-twenties or early thirties, ca. 1865–70. (Bauduin Collection)*

saburo and the author Muramatsu Shofu. During the discussion
between these two men, Muramatsu asked Guraba whether his
mother was the real model for Madame Butterfly and Guraba,
said Ikegami, nodded in an affirmative way. Commenting on this
event, Ikegami mentioned to Noda how surprised he had been
about Guraba's affirmation since, as he told Noda, "Mr. Glover
was by no means fickle like Pinkerton" (referring to Guraba's
presumed father Thomas B. Glover and demonstrating how
familiar he was with the Butterfly story). The story was not published by Muramatsu but it appeared in the press a few times
after the publication of Noda's book in 1972.

So we have here two witnesses: Miura Tamaki, based on Long,
and Ikegami, based on Guraba Tomisaburo. But more verification
is needed before assuming that Tom Glover's mother is the real-
life model of the Butterfly Mrs. Correll talked to her brother
about in 1897. When we dig a little bit into the history of the
"Tom Glover" to whom Miura Tamaki and Noda Heinosuke
referred, we find that in reality he was not the natural son of
Awajiya Tsuru, as has often been assumed, but of a woman called
Kaga Maki.[8] At the time of her son's birth, she lived in Nagasaki's Konyamachi, a downtown area located partially on a hill
(another "opposite hill" from Higashi Yamate) and, unlike Awajiya Tsuru, she went through the combined experiences of having
a child with a foreign man, being abandoned by that man, and

giving up the child to that man's family at a later date. There are still more details of her life to be examined, but one can assume at this point that Kaga Maki, the mother of Tom Glover, is the real model for Madame Butterfly.

Why has this simple fact not been more often and more generally acknowledged? Why have much less documented guesses proliferated? The most likely answer is that Miura Tamaki's story remained, for a long time, her own personal and unconfirmed version of the real facts. The confirmation by Guraba Tomisaburo, which was part of Noda's 1972 book, has been systematically kept out of sight by those in Japan who suspected that the Butterfly story would absorb the attention of the public to the detriment of the real economic and political importance of Guraba's presumed father, Thomas B. Glover, in early Meiji Japan. As far as I can see, the original version of Noda's story has never even been translated. Thus, Noda's innocent but accurate simple notes on what he heard and saw in Nagasaki have remained

*Thomas B. Glover, ca. 1895. (Nagasaki Prefectural Library)*

hidden and have not received the attention they deserve. His rendering of the discussion with Ikegami Heizo strikes me as an
uncomplicated and authentic story.

Guraba Tomisaburo's original name was Shinsaburo and his
birth on 8 December 1870 is registered (with the clear indication of Kaga Maki as his natural mother) on the *koseki* (family
register) of Awajiya Tsuru, his adoptive mother. In 1877 Kaga
Maki married a Japanese and moved away. In 1888 she divorced
and returned to Nagasaki, where she died in 1906.

Sometime before his mother moved away with her husband in
1877, the six-year-old Shinsaburo was removed from her house
and passed on to the household of Awajiya Tsuru, who lived on
the Kojimamachi hill in a house belonging to Thomas B. Glover.
Tsuru was born in 1849 in Osaka as the daughter of Otsuki
Fumisuke. She was adopted by Awajiya Yasubei, who had a small
shipyard in Osaka, and his wife Sato. In 1862 she married a
samurai of the Takeda clan, Yamamura Kunitaro, and moved with
him to Hogo-Takeda. They had a daughter, Sen, born in 1863.
Shortly afterward she and her husband divorced and Tsuru went
back to Osaka without her child. For a number of years, she then
made a living as a *yujo* in the Kagai inn in Osaka's Kitahama section. Around 1868 she met Thomas B. Glover there and followed him to Nagasaki. When around 1876 or 1877 Shinsaburo
joined her household, he took her family name: Awajiya. The boy

visited the Cobleigh Seminary, established by Caroll Long (no relation to John Luther Long) in 1881 as a missionary school and predecessor of Chinzei Gakkan, which Irvin Correll would become a headmaster of later on. A few years later, Shinsaburo was pursuing his studies at the prestigious Gakushuin, an upper-class university-level college in Tokyo, where he graduated in 1888. That year he officially changed his name to Tomisaburo, a fact that has been registered on Tsuru's *koseki* together with the confirmation of his adoption by her at an earlier but unspec-ified date. We lose track of him during the next two years but he resurfaces in 1891, when he registered as "Tomi-saburo Awajiya Glover of To-kyo, Japan" at the University of Pennsylvania in Philadel-phia for a two-year course in biology and natural history. He returned to Japan without graduating.

*Portrait of Thomas Glover's wife, Awa-jiya Tsuru, and her adopted daughter, Nakano Waka. (Nagasaki Prefectural Library)*

Tomisaburo's family history is important not only to estab-lish his relationships with his natural and adoptive mothers but also to explore his ties with the Glover family, which became relevant after his adoption by Awajiya Tsuru. Glover's "wife" Tsuru, who in 1876 (approximately the time she started taking care of Tomisaburo) had given birth to her daughter Hana, adopted in 1890 a girl called Nakano Waka, born in 1875 as the youngest daughter of Nakano Ei of Yokohama and James Walter, an English merchant in that city who was well acquainted with the Glover family in Nagasaki. In 1894 Tsuru had her own childhood adoption by Awajiya Yasubei registered on her *koseki*, where it had been omitted by mistake when she moved to Nagasaki in 1868. Although in 1894 she already lived with Thomas B. Glover in Tokyo, she temporarily moved back that same year to Nagasaki and registered at Ebisu-cho 33. She was joined there a few months later by her adopted son Tomisaburo, who had taken up a position with the trading house of Holme, Ringer and Co. and "reestablished" the family register of the "extinct" Guraba family.

As such a lineage in reality did not exist, this "reopening" of a *koseki* simply meant that he managed (necessarily with the help of influential authorities) to change the name Awajiya into a name with a solid Japanese samurai family connotation and, in the process, into the Japanese phonetic equivalent of the name Glover. Because he fixed his residence at the same address as Tsuru and her daughters in Ebisu-cho 33, the change of name must

*Thomas Glover's bungalow Ippon-matsu in Nagasaki toward the end of the nineteenth century. (Nagasaki Prefectural Library)*

be seen as a deliberate decision to establish a Japanese branch of the Glover family, now called Guraba. The new branch consisted of Tomisaburo as head of the family, his "sisters" Hana and Waka, and his adoptive mother Tsuru, all living at Ebisu-cho 33, Nagasaki.[9] Two years later, Tomisaburo adopted his sister Hana, who thus obtained a registered "father" who in 1897 could marry her as his "daughter" Guraba Hana to Walter George Bennett, the future British consul in Inshon, Korea. (The final step in Hana's renaming came after her death in 1938 when her hus-

*Wedding of Guraba Hana and Walter Bennett in 1897. The photograph was taken in front of Thomas Glover's bungalow Ippon-matsu. In the center back row are Thomas Glover and Tsuru, and somewhat to the right, in the background, wearing glasses, is Guraba Tomisaburo. (Nagasaki Prefectural Library)*

band recorded her name on her tombstone in Inshon as Hana Glover.)

Meanwhile Tomisaburo started a sort of double life. He kept his Japanese address in Ebisu-cho but had himself also registered in the annual lists of foreigners in Japan under the name T. A. Glover. From 1894 until 1897 his address was at the office of Holme, Ringer and Co. in Nagasaki, and after 1897 it was Minami Yamate Number 3, the house known as Ippon-matsu (literally, "One Pine Tree," after the single pine tree that pierced the roof of the greenhouse), which was built in 1863 by Thomas B. Glover, who had lived there until 1887 and still occupied it intermittently after moving to Tokyo. Thomas B. Glover had sold the house to the Mitsubishi Company in 1888, so Tomisaburo was therefore a tenant of Mitsubishi. The wedding of Hana and Walter Bennett in 1897 took place there, and presumably also the one between Tomisaburo and Waka (brother and sister through adoption!) that took place in 1899—a low-key event because Tsuru had died early that year and was buried in Nagasaki's Taiheiji Temple cemetery. Tomisaburo and Waka lived in Ippon-matsu until 1906, then moved to Minami Yamate Number 9 at the foot of the same hill.

Between 1894 (Tomisaburo's return to Nagasaki) and 1911 (the year Thomas B. Glover died), he and Waka were known in the foreign community as Mr. and Mrs.

*Undated photograph (ca. 1910–20) of Guraba Tomisaburo (dressed up as an officer of the U.S. Navy), taken during a fancy dress party in Nagasaki. (Nagasaki Prefectural Library)*

*Right to left: Thomas B. Glover, Guraba Tomisaburo, Hana Bennett, and Guraba Waka. One of Hana's children is in the foreground. Ca. 1910 in Tokyo. (Nagasaki Prefectural Library)*

Thomas A. Glover, the name under which they also appeared in the annual list of foreigners. After Thomas B. Glover's death their names disappeared from the list but they continued being registered, like normal Japanese citizens, in the *koseki* under the name of Guraba until both died and the *koseki* was canceled. They belonged in a way to the local bourgeoisie and hosted parties for both Japanese and foreigners. There is a picture of Tomisaburo showing up at a fancy dress ball in the uniform of an American navy officer—sometimes interpreted as hinting at Lieutenant Pinkerton! But when problems arose, they were not really considered Japanese any longer; during World War II they found themselves increasingly isolated. Waka died in 1943 of tuberculosis and Tomisaburo took his life a few days after the capitulation of Japan in 1945.[10]

## TOM GLOVER'S FATHER

At this point, there are three things that we can consider to be facts. First, according to John Luther Long and Guraba Tomisaburo, the latter's mother is the real-life model for Madame Butterfly and this person can only be Kaga Maki—Tomisaburo's natural mother—not Tsuru, who was never abandoned by her lover. Second, the story of the child having to be given up by the mother (which is not mentioned by Jennie Correll but occurs in Long's novel, in Belasco's play, and in the opera) turns out to have happened in real life. Third, there is a clear link between the story and the Glover family. That brings us to the next question: who was the father? The question is not as important as the issue of Kaga Maki being the model for Madame Butterfly and her son's identification with Trouble, because Long's lieutenant is largely copied from Loti and certainly not from an American navy officer.[11] But it would be useful to know whether the child's father played a part that at any time could have contributed to the story being brought to Jennie Correll's attention.

It is generally assumed that Thomas B. Glover, the British merchant of Nagasaki, was Tomisaburo's father because his common-law wife Tsuru adopted the boy and because in his last will and testament of 1907 he names as his heirs "Hana and Tomisabro" [*sic*]. Moreover, the numerous Glover family photo albums kept in Nagasaki present Tomisaburo clearly as the oldest child of the Glover family. Taking into account the family history as described above there is little doubt that he was a Glover. But was Thomas B. Glover his father?

There were three Glovers in Nagasaki in 1870, the year Tomisaburo was born. Thomas Blake Glover, born in Aberdeen in 1838 and a resident of Japan since 1859, was the most famous of them. He was a Scottish merchant and entrepreneur who, in spite of serious failures (he went into bankruptcy in 1870 because of bad planning and bad management of a coal mine on a small island off the coast near Nagasaki), played a not unimportant role in the economic development of Japan while it was entering into modern times. He also supplied useful intelligence to the British diplomats as well as to the daimyo of the western clans of Japan when they were plotting against the reign of the shogun. Until 1887 he was a resident of Nagasaki; from then on he mainly lived in Tokyo, where he died in 1911. His remains were buried in Nagasaki's Sakamoto International Cemetery.

He had two brothers who were often closely associated with him. His younger brother Alex was born in Aberdeen in 1840 and arrived in Japan in 1864. In 1866 he married Ann Finlay in Nagasaki, where she had followed him from Scotland. She gave birth, that same year, to stillborn twins and shortly afterward she and her husband returned to Scotland. Alex then came back to Japan in 1869 and stayed in Nagasaki until 1874, when he moved to Shanghai. In 1882 he went to America and apparently remained there for the rest of his life without ever having been in contact again with his wife in Europe.

The other brother, the youngest of the Glover family, was Alfred. He was born in 1850 in Bridge of Don in Scotland and came to Nagasaki in 1868 to work with Thomas. After his brother's bankruptcy was

*Photograph taken in 1867 in Aberdeen of the six Glover brothers. Thomas is seated at the right, Alex is standing behind him, and Alfred is leaning over the table at the left. (Nagasaki Prefectural Library)*

*Foreigners in Glover Garden, Nagasaki, around 1865. Second from left is Thomas Glover.
At the extreme right is Alfred Glover, and seated next to him is Alex Glover. (Bauduin
Collection)*

canceled in 1877, Alfred worked for other companies and eventually was enrolled in 1878 by the office of Holme, Ringer and
Co. in Nagasaki. He stayed there when Thomas moved to Tokyo
in 1887. In 1894 he was joined at his company by Guraba
Tomisaburo. Alfred intended to go back to Scotland in 1904 but
on the way home he died in Hong Kong. His body was returned

to Nagasaki, where he was buried in the Sakamoto International Cemetery.

Which of the three brothers could have been Tomisaburo's father? To father a child born on 8 December 1870 with a mother living in Nagasaki, a man should have been physically present in that city around the first half of March 1870. We happen to know Thomas B. Glover's whereabouts early that year: he left Nagasaki in the middle of January for Shanghai, where he had discussions with the directors of Jardine Matheson and Co., the Far East trading company that he hoped to convince to financially rescue his coal mine venture. Copies of the correspondence between Thomas B. Glover, Jardine Matheson and Co., and the Dutch Trading Society (also interested in the mine) show that Glover was in Shanghai in January and February and in Hyogo (present-day Kobe) during most of March. There is no proof that on his journey from Shanghai to Hyogo he did or did not pass through Nagasaki, but given the vital importance and the urgency of solving his problems as well as the time needed to travel from one place to another, it is unlikely that he did. And even in the unlikely case that he passed through Nagasaki, it could only have been very briefly and without either the time or the mood for relaxing adventures.

Alex and Alfred, however, were both in Nagasaki during the early part of 1870 and either one could have fathered the child.

The fact that it was eventually Thomas's companion Tsuru who adopted the child is not necessarily an indication of Thomas's fatherhood: the boy was a Glover and neither Alex, who had a bad marriage and whose wife had serious health problems, nor Alfred, who was unmarried, young, and volatile, could guarantee the kind of upbringing that would be possible with Tsuru's care and Thomas's supervision. Thomas B. Glover was known to be a generous man; he took good care of his daughter Hana, the only survivor of his own four children, and agreed to adopt his friend's daughter Waka (a long time before there was any question of Waka's marriage with Tomisaburo).[12] Also, there was already the beginning of a kind of regular family life between Thomas and Tsuru, who started living permanently in the same house sometime after the birth of Hana in 1876. There was no boy in the family and Tomisaburo's adoption must have felt logical even if Thomas was not the father. Most likely, Alfred was the real father because he had the closest links with Tomisaburo: Tomisaburo stayed with him when the others moved to Tokyo, he joined the same company as Alfred, and he took care of Alfred's funeral when he died abroad. But this is not certain. If Jennie Correll's mention of a departure of the father by ship was part of the original story she was told, the father could also have been Alex, who left Nagasaki in 1874, when Tomisaburo was three years old, and never came back.

## More Clues

This brings us back to the question of the timing of the story. Clearly it cannot have taken place during the period of the Corrells' stay in Nagasaki, because when they arrived in 1892, Tomisaburo was already twenty-one years old and a student in Philadelphia. Jennie Correll must have referred to an event that she had not experienced herself but heard secondhand, perhaps from her "usual shopkeeper," as she told her Japanese audience in 1931. Surprisingly, Jennie gave an accurate clue to the timing in an interview in Shanghai, also in 1931, when she said that Cho-san was living "very near their home in Nagasaki, when they first arrived in Japan."[13] We know that the Corrells arrived in Japan in 1873. To bring up in 1897 (the year she mentioned it to her brother) a story that happened about twenty years before her arrival in Nagasaki makes sense only if Mrs. Correll had picked up in the gossiping community of Nagasaki (which must have included her shopkeeper!) one or more facts that had given new life to an old story.

And that was exactly what happened. The period 1894 to 1897 was full of events in the life of the Glover family and their dependents. In 1894 Tomisaburo came back to Nagasaki to take up residence, open a new *koseki*, and start a job. In 1896 Hana returned from Tokyo and was adopted by her stepbrother. That same year Thomas B. Glover, who had lived in Tokyo since 1887, settled in Nagasaki again for one year, a move for which the motives are not known. Early in 1897, Hana married in Nagasaki. The Glover family photo albums show that during those years members of the Kaga family (but not Maki) joined the Glovers/Gurabas at some occasions. There can be no doubt that all this was more than enough reason for excitement and gossip in a small provincial town with a mixed population. Whether Jennie Correll's imperfect rendering of the events was due to her insufficient knowledge of the Japanese language or her personal sense of drama remains unknown. But the identification of Tomisaburo/Tom Glover and his mother Kaga Maki with Trouble and Butterfly could only have been confirmed by Long if his sister or her husband had told him, because Long had no direct links with Nagasaki and never went there.

That leaves one final question: why would Jennie Correll call Tomisaburo's mother "Cho-san"? An easy answer is that she picked a random name that would hide the identity of a person who at the time of the writing of the short story was still alive and living in Nagasaki. Another easy answer is that Long took the name from Loti or Messager (who has some elaborate verse on a dying butterfly, sung by Chrysanthème). But I think there is a more realistic explanation. There is little doubt that Kaga Maki was working in the entertainment business, not only because Jennie called her a "tea-house girl" but also because foreign men normally would not meet Japanese women of other social categories. Women working in the pleasure quarters of the cities would generally (both then and today) assume a poetic pseudonym to use with their customers. O-Cho-san (Honorable Miss Butterfly) was a typical nom de guerre for a person in the business and it would be normal to refer to her that way. Actually, it is quite possible that Mrs. Correll never even knew her real name.

Mrs. Oyama may have been referring to the same story when she talked to Puccini. She lived in Tokyo and had no ties with Nagasaki, but her father, Nomura Motosuke, a samurai of the Choshu clan, had, after the Meiji Restoration, become an official of the Ministry of Education and was in charge of the inspection of schools. Between May and July of 1876 he was in Kyushu to inspect schools and Nagasaki must have been on his itinerary.[14] If Mrs. Oyama knew a story "exactly like Butterfly's" (as she told Puccini), it must have been her father who had brought it home from Nagasaki. Being involved in school problems, he would have been informed of the case of a half-Japanese child being claimed by a foreigner who had been such a close business associate of his clan during previous years and whose bankruptcy was such a notorious case. But we'll never know with certainty if her story was the same as Jennie's.

Even without the support of Mrs. Oyama's story, the conclusion remains the same: the story Jennie Correll heard in Nagasaki during her last years there concerned past events in the Glover family, which had a high profile in Nagasaki. She was vague about details because it was an old story surrounded by local gossip, and she heard it in a language she probably was not very fluent in. But the main facts were clear and she told her brother John Luther Long (who in turn told Miura Tamaki) who Butterfly's son was. Her brother also mentioned that Jennie knew Tom Glover, which is not surprising; she must have taken pride in meeting Tomisaburo when he came back to Nagasaki in 1894 because he was one of the four oldest Nagasaki pupils of her school. Tomisaburo himself saw no reason not to give a positive reply when Muramatsu Shofu asked him the question that others would have liked to ask him too: are you really Butterfly's son?[15]

*Opera in the narrow sense was
a form which it was thought
necessary to have if Japan was
to be civilized and enlightened.*

EDWARD SEIDENSTICKER

# 6

## *"Madama Butterfly" in Japan*

WITH SO MANY ROOTS IN JAPAN, ONE WOULD EXPECT PUCCINI'S *Madama Butterfly* to rank among the most successful operas in Japan, a country in which European operas generally are very popular. Nothing is less true. The opera did gradually become accepted by the public, but only after long hesitation and with much reserve. When performed, it might shock or sadden the audience but it certainly does not reach the degree of popularity of, for example, Verdi's *La Traviata* or its literary predecessor, Dumas's *La Dame aux Camélias* (better known in Japan under her Japanese name: Tsubaki-hime, the Camellia Princess). Both operas feature in the title role a woman of dubious background and morality and focus on the central theme of this woman's sacrifice of herself for a man who chose (or is believed to have chosen) another life. It is the sacrifice of the woman, much more than the un-Japanese contrast between pure love and mere pleasure, however refined, that finds recognition in Japan. Tsubaki-hime conveys that feature more clearly than Butterfly, whose Japaneseness, combined with her submission to the will of a foreign, Caucasian man, complicates the message rather than clarifying it in the eyes of a Japanese public. The only attraction of the Japanese element of the story is the flattering fact of a foreign novel with a plot set in Japan and turned into a popular opera by a famous European composer; this aspect has, of course, little to do with artistic appreciation and is on par with the statues and memorial stones erected in honor of Pierre Loti and Giacomo Puccini in Nagasaki.

The little esteem for *Madama Butterfly* in Japan is clearly shown by the history of its performances in that country. Of course, opera, as a form of Western musical expression, came late to Japan. The first one ever was a Japanese version of the German composer Christoph Willibald Gluck's *Orfeo ed Euridice*, performed in 1903 by students of the Tokyo Musical School, among them a still very young Miura Tamaki. In 1912 the Imperial Theatre in Tokyo engaged G. V. Rossi, an Italian musician and impresario, for the purpose of familiarizing the Japanese public with Western opera.[1] Rossi worked for the Imperial Theatre until 1916 and produced, among others, Mozart's *The Magic Flute* with an all-Japanese cast, and several Italian operas.

Attention was drawn, naturally, to *Madama Butterfly*, but the earliest performances show that the public was extremely hesitant to deal with the issues it raised. The first attempt to present the work took place in 1914 in the Imperial Theatre in Tokyo, at a time when Rossi was still there. At that occasion, part of the opera was performed, but not the dramatic ending. It was followed by a program of Japanese songs that seemed to be needed to turn around the mood of an audience embarrassed by the "contemptuous glance at the customs and habits of loose women" in Japan, as the *Asahi Shimbun* wrote. The author of the article was apparently more concerned by the erroneous impressions foreigners have of Japanese customs and the fact that this misinformed concept is reproduced on the stage of such a prestigious place as the Imperial Theatre, than by the habits of "loose women" as such.

## Untraditional Versions of the Opera

Kawakami Sadayakko, whose interest in the subject must have been strengthened by her meeting with Puccini in Milan in 1902, converted the opera into a theater play (rather than reverting to Belasco's play), which was performed in 1916 in Osaka. She did everything possible to make her interpretation look like a foreign production. She played Butterfly herself, and the American roles were taken up by foreign actors. The child Trouble was renamed Yoneo, a name that suggests an American origin (the character *yone*, for "rice," is also pronounced *bei* and is used as a kind of syllabic shorthand for "America"). The same play was performed in the Imperial Theatre in Tokyo in 1917 with some of Puccini's music. It had obvious antiforeign accents and appeared to be sending a warning to Japanese women not to mingle with foreign men. One newspaper reported that many women in the audience cried. Following publication of a short, rather distorted rendering of the story in 1921 in *Fujin Koron*, a women's magazine, and the successful launching of the score of a "Madame Butterfly Fox-Trot" for violin and mandolin in 1926, the story returned to the stage in 1930 in the form of a new version of the play, peformed, again, with fragments of Puccini's music. This time the text leaned more heavily on Loti's *Madame Chrysanthème* but also borrowed from the libretto of Puccini's opera.

The opera itself was performed in 1924 in Osaka and Kyoto and in 1930 in Tokyo with a large number of cuts and other changes and with foreigners singing foreign roles in English. This reduced version, wrote the *Hochi Shimbun,* could be seen by the Japanese "with peace of mind." As on earlier occasions, this peace of mind was assured by eliminating possible offenses to national pride—for example, the use of the Japanese national anthem and the military song "Miya sama"—while being indifferent to Butterfly's personal predicaments. The latter seemed to be relevant only under the aspect of the symbolic meaning for foreign abuse of Japanese virtues.

The first production in Japan of the complete version of Puccini's *Madama Butterfly* finally took place in 1936, thirty years after the Parisian performance of the opera as we know it today. That year Miura Tamaki, who had already sung the title role two thousand times abroad, gave her first performance in Japan as Cho-Cho-san in the authentic version of the opera at the Tokyo Kabukiza.

Obviously, the war years were not favorable for this kind of entertainment and only after 1945, and with the encouragement of the American occupation forces, did performances of the opera start again. However, mediocre and trivial comedies and musicals based on the *Butterfly* story were always more numerous than the presentations of the original. Among these derivative

versions is a Bunraku (puppet play) production in the puppet
theater of Osaka in 1956, which, according to the printed program (and not unexpectedly), was "quite different from the original opera itself" and contained "some passages that are not
necessarily true to the original." The time of the performance
was reduced to one hour and five minutes from the original two
hours and fifteen minutes. The story itself was converted into
something close to classical Japanese drama.

Because of its shocking aspects and in spite of the pleasure
some take in the sentimentality of the story, the original *Madama
Butterfly* today still meets limited enthusiasm in Japan and continues to be deviated in various directions. Even when it is staged
with integrity by a Japanese opera company such as Fujiwara
(that is, sung in Italian by Japanese singers), it still acquires the
unmistakable patina of the cheap drama as it is produced in the
theaters of the *takarazuka* style that is so popular in Osaka and
Tokyo. The opera prompts signs of embarrassment within the
audience both with regard to certain scenes that are supposed to
be Japanese and because of the use of "Kimigayo," the national
anthem. There are, however, more profound reasons for the feelings of discomfort that Japanese audiences have when they see
this opera; it is, after all, a story set in Japan but seen through
Western eyes.

# How Japanese Is It?

There are numerous authentically Japanese elements in the opera. Everything observed and noted by Loti and carried on by Long, together with Mrs. Correll's observations and Long's own readings, supplies direct impressions of the mixed world of Japanese and foreigners in Nagasaki, and Puccini's librettists served themselves abundantly from those sources. The opera is full of big and small details that are entirely Japanese: the sliding walls, the small house made of wood and paper, the view from the hillside on the bay of Nagasaki, the parasols, the bowing, Yakuside's low tolerance for alcohol, Butterfly's small belongings carried in her sleeves, the wedding taking place at the house, the sword carrying a message on the blade, and the exclusion from the Japanese community for being suspected of being Christian. It is also interesting to note that Butterfly expects Pinkerton to return in a "white ship" as opposed to the notorious "black ships" in which Commodore Perry arrived in 1854.

Not all names are authentic. Starting with those mentioned by Long, "Cio-Cio-san" (Cho-Cho-san) is a correct name for a girl working in the entertainment quarter; and "Suzuki" and "Goro" are normal family names. "Yamadori," however, is a very unusual name and to Japanese ears even a ridiculous one for a retired daimyo, because the word literally means "mountain bird" and indicates a Japanese variety of the pheasant; the Japanese *Who's Who* does not list a single person under that name. As for other names or words, we do not know where Puccini's team found them, but in a letter to Giulio Ricordi of late summer 1902, Puccini mentions that he discussed them with Mrs. Oyama; she advised him on some of them and could well have suggested some new ones, such as "Omara" ("Omura" would be better), as a section of Nagasaki, and Surandasico (in the curse of the bonze), which could be a garbled reading of the word *zurugashikoi* (meaning "cunning").

The names of the government officials (in the Milan version) have luckily been eliminated from the final libretto: "Hanako" is a very unusual name—in fact, it is a first name for a girl; "Takasago" is, more appropriately, a musical phrase of the Noh theater that expresses good wishes, especially for a wedding. The name "Yakuside" (originally it was "Yaxonpidé") vaguely suggests "causing misfortune." The Japanese words used in the libretto sometimes are authentic, such as in the case where the family toasts to the newlywed couple and says "*okami*," which is an old-fashioned expression meaning "housewife." Uncle Yakuside's song (which was also cut) mentions the "*goseki*," or "registration act," but most of what he sings is gibberish.

References to Japanese religion give a confused picture. Puccini successfully captured the mixture of Buddhism and Shinto so typical for Japan, but he was frequently mistaken with regard to details. The *hotoke*, for example, is a Buddhist notion that indicates the enlightened state of the souls of the departed. Loti was close to the truth in calling them spirits of ancestors. Long speaks of living and dead ancestors. Puccini turns them into statues of ancestors for whom Pinkerton, jokingly, bows; then Butterfly throws them away.[2] This last gesture was deleted in the final version of the opera, but the implication of ridicule and Butterfly's willingness to give up traditional Japanese concepts remains. This is confirmed immediately afterward by the readiness she expresses to become a Christian. Her interruption of Suzuki's prayers at the beginning of act 2 with insults addressed to the Japanese gods is meant to convey the same idea of a separation with Japanese traditions. The same applies to the next scene where Butterfly mentions the locks, which Pinkerton had fixed on the front door, as a clear indication of his return: as Lafcadio Hearn notes, "No ordinary person can shut his door to lock out the rest of the world. Everybody's house must be open to visitors; to close its gates by day would be regarded as an insult to the community. . . ." Locking the door emphasizes Butterfly's conscious isolation from her Japanese surroundings. For a Japanese audience, familiar since the beginning of the opera with how utterly unrealistic Butterfly is about her marriage with Pinkerton, there is overall very little reason to admire her character or attitudes. While there is in Japan a sincere admiration for a person embodying the tragic hero, this does not apply to Butterfly, who is neither a hero nor unequivocally tragic.[3] At most, her tragedy is the consequence of her own blatant mistakes.

That is the most fundamental problem for a Japanese understanding of Butterfly. When she arrives on the scene in act I, she tells her friends that she is "the happiest girl of Japan" and that she comes "at love's summons." At that time, the audience already knows that she has been bought for a hundred yen out of an "assortment" (including one of her cousins), that the contract can be annulled, and that her family knows (or hopes) that she will be divorced again at the end. Here, Butterfly, behaving like a shy girl bride entering the nuptial room for the wedding night, reveals her naiveté. She is aware of the risks of a relationship with a Western man because of cultural differences ("We are people accustomed to little things, humble and silent, to a tenderness, barely grazing and yet deep as the sky, as the sea's wave," she warns Pinkerton) but does not seem to take the nature of the contract into account. Western audiences accept Butterfly's change of mind and heart after she meets Pinkerton in person, and they understand the conclusions she draws from that encounter at least for her own conduct; but in Japanese eyes her position is utterly unrealistic.

Even in entirely normal, regular cases, and as recently as the end of the nineteenth century, which is the timing of the opera's story, the position of women in the Japanese family appeared to be "the reverse of happy": they lived in a state of subjection, could be divorced at any time, and in that event lost their claim on the children.[4] To believe that a woman's love can become a force that will save her from her fate is a totally alien notion in Japan, and to think that this can be done on the basis of a prostitution contract with a foreigner is foolhardy.

It is not the contract that shocks the audiences but the state of mind of the woman who signs it. That is one of the main reasons *Madama Butterfly* embarrasses Japanese audiences and why the story has so often been cut down to shorter proportions with a more conformist content—or simply turned into a farce. Also, whenever the original version is performed, Butterfly's *jigai* suicide at the end (perfectly in style for a woman of a samurai background), sad as it is, forms the best denouement one could wish, the only one that brings to a final end a melodrama mixed with ridicule.

## *Madama Butterfly* Today

Miura Tamaki did everything possible to popularize *Madama Butterfly* in Japan, and when she died in 1946 (after difficult war years when the official opinion held her in low esteem) her work

*The Japanese soprano Miura Tamaki (1884–1946), who performed the role of Madama Butterfly more than 2,000 times worldwide and who introduced Puccini's opera to Japan in 1936.*

was continued by the soprano Kobayashi Nobue until her death in 1976. The latter founded the Miura Tamaki Memorial Association in 1952. She is the person who was responsible for the Butterfly statue in honor of Miura Tamaki in Nagasaki's Glover Garden, and she also had a stone butterfly erected in her memory in the cemetery of the Kaneiji temple in Tokyo's Ueno ward. In 1967, Kobayashi Nobue launched the first of a series of "Worldwide *Madama Butterfly* Competition" performances that since that time have taken place at regular intervals. This tradition was interrupted after Mrs. Kobayashi's death, but was taken up again in 1986 by Mr. Nakajima Shinkichi, who manages this big event from his modest office on Aoyama Dori in Tokyo. The competition brings together, at a place somewhere in America or Europe, a great number of young singers. The prizewinners give a final recital in Glover Garden in Nagasaki, where the leading soprano performs "Un bel di vedremmo" dressed in the red kimono that once was used by Miura Tamaki during her performances in the twenties and thirties, when she traveled the world as the Japanese Cio-Cio-san. But her success in the world was never matched in Japan, and Mr. Nakajima's intimate and sympathetic recital in Nagasaki resembles nothing more than a harmless cult.

# *Afterword*

CLEARLY, THE MAIN CHARACTER OF PUCCINI'S *Madama Butterfly* is an unrealistic, if not irrational, woman. The success of the opera is carried by her stimulating personality and by Puccini's capacity to translate human thoughts and feelings into a musical language of beauty and clarity that many understand. But the intrigue is weak because of the lack of realism of the heroine and her lopsided logic. Butterfly's change of heart when she sees Pinkerton for the first time (an event we do not see firsthand) might be understandable but her expectation that Pinkerton will reciprocate her love and be her loyal husband is an unexplainable error of judgment. This fundamental defect was present in Long's novel and was carried over into the opera without any serious effort to correct or explain it. In the libretto, Butterfly remains incapable of understanding the irreconcilable contradiction between her real feelings for Pinkerton and the contract they signed. Her real tragedy is that she does not grasp the immensity of her mistake, which then leads to the unavoidable final disaster. Certainly, Butterfly's personality is as attractive as it is dignified but her misperception of reality is unbelievably naive.

There is no record that shows whether Puccini was aware of this substantive weakness but we do know how he dealt with the problem of the opera's form. He visualized the opera on the basis of Belasco's play and, for reasons analyzed earlier in this book, he wanted to stay as close as possible to it. He was so stubborn in that conviction that he forgot some of the basic requirements of theater and opera, ignored the advice of his closest collaborators, and persisted in wrapping the entire contents of the play (and more) into a single act 2. The fiasco of the premiere of *Madama Butterfly* at La Scala was at least partly a consequence of his obstinacy (successfully exploited by an active anti-Puccini lobby). The later success of the modified opera is an indication that the initial disaster could have been avoided. How much this episode must have shaken his artistic judgment becomes clear when we observe his later dealings with Albert Carré and Tito Ricordi

*Portrait of "Tom Glover" (alias Guraba Tomisaburo) in his school uniform at about age fifteen. (Nagasaki Prefectural Library)*

regarding further changes in the opera: first, he categorically rejected their suggestions, then accepted nearly all of them. Even if in its final shape the opera is a better product than its initial version, the fact remains that Puccini made a fundamental mistake in a creative field where he was the master.

Another real-life tragedy occurred in Nagasaki. We do not know enough details about the relationship between Kaga Maki, the original Butterfly, and the Glover (one of the three brothers; we don't know for certain which) who fathered her child, or about the circumstances under which the father left and the child was claimed by his family, to make a fair assessment of the nature of the early roots of the opera's story in the gossip Mrs. Correll heard during her stay in Nagasaki. But Tomisaburo, the model for Butterfly's child Trouble (Dolore, the name that would be changed into Gioia—Joy—when his father returned), remained marked by the tragedy of his youth throughout his entire life. His alienation was already unmistakable at a very young age. When as an eleven year old, back in 1881, he visited the Cobleigh Seminary, he is described by a witness as shy and withdrawn. Pictures from Nagasaki and Tokyo show him dressed in school uniform or formal Japanese *haori* and *hakama* (the short kimono and pleated skirt used for formal occasions) always looking shy, introverted, serious, or depressed: a Eurasian child dressed as a Japanese. Only around the age of twenty does he start dressing in Western suits. His traveling abroad to America and Scotland (where he met the rest of the Glover family) must have made him more aware of his position between the two worlds. Eventually, he opted for being Japanese: when the last male Glover in Japan died in 1911, Tomisaburo's name disappeared from the annual lists of foreign residents.

He was a successful businessman in Nagasaki and enjoyed what appeared to be a normal social life with friends and family.[1] But when the period came that Richard Storry called "The Dark Valley," Tomisaburo and his wife Waka and one other mixed family, the Walkers, began a period of near total isolation.[2] The last known photograph of Tomisaburo shows him in November 1941, seated with a few Mitsubishi directors in front of Ipponmatsu; he looks worn out and depressed and wears an old saggy suit, and his big dramatic eyes look into the camera with an expression of immense sadness.

After Waka's death in 1943 he lived alone with an old Japanese maid in his house at the foot of Minami Yamate. When in August 1945 the nuclear bomb fell on Urakami in the north of Nagasaki, several weeks of total chaos followed with thousands of dying refugees on the roads along the bay. In the middle of that inferno, young Albert Walker was sent by his father to Tomisaburo's house. When Albert arrived, he found the door unlocked and the maid gone. A giant black American soldier was cutting Tomisaburo's cold body loose from the rope.[3]

An old Nagasaki man, Kosone Kinjiro, wrote the obituary. He wrote that Tomisaburo had felt that he was a Japanese and that he killed himself "because he suffered from being considered as half foreign." This was Tomisaburo's tragedy: he thought he was Japanese but in reality he was stuck between two worlds. He remained Butterfly's child. His name was Trouble, and the time never came that it was changed into Joy.

# *Puccini's "Madama Butterfly" Plot Summary*

*Note*: Square brackets indicate portions deleted in the final version.

## Act I

Lieutenant Pinkerton of the U.S. Navy is inspecting his newly rented house on a hillside overlooking Nagasaki. He is assisted by Goro, who has arranged the lease as well as Pinkerton's marriage to Madama Butterfly, a Japanese geisha. Goro presents the servants [whom Pinkerton ridicules] and gives explanations about Butterfly's family and the coming events. The U.S. consul Sharpless arrives. In their discussion, Pinkerton boasts of his hedonistic "Yankee vagabondo" style, which Sharpless disagrees with. Pinkerton mentions his lease and his marriage, both concluded for 999 years but leaving him free to annul monthly. They toast America. Goro praises the beauty of the bride, whose price was only a hundred yen. Pinkerton describes her Japanese appearance and expresses his excitement. Sharpless reports on Butterfly's visit to the consulate and warns Pinkerton that she takes it seriously, but Pinkerton ignores his admonitions. They toast again, this time to Pinkerton's future real marriage with a real American bride.

Butterfly and her friends can be heard as they approach the house; she comes, she says, at love's summons and is the happiest girl in Japan. They enter and exchange bows. When questioned by Sharpless, Butterfly explains that she is from a once-wealthy Nagasaki family; now she is poor and she became a geisha to make a living. She has a mother but no sisters and her father has died. [She claims two uncles: a bonze and a drunk, which provokes Pinkerton to some sarcastic comments.] She confesses that she is fifteen years old. [Pinkerton makes more sarcastic remarks about servants, food, and the drinks that are offered.]

The Japanese officials arrive, together with relatives: Butterfly's mother, aunt, cousins, and her Uncle Yakuside. They discuss Pinkerton's appearance. One cousin mentions that she refused him when he was first offered to her but she is corrected by Butterfly. Some friends expect a divorce. Uncle Yakuside inspects the drinks. Sharpless warns Pinkerton again that Butterfly takes the situation seriously. [Goro tips the officials "the American way." Butterfly presents her relatives. Sharpless presents "Sir Francis Blummy Pinkerton" to the officials.] Butterfly shows Pinkerton her knick-knacks: handkerchief, pipe, sash, brooch, mirror, fan, and a jar of paint (which she throws away). Goro explains the other object: a sword that the Mikado gave her father to commit suicide. Finally, Butterfly shows the ottoke, to whom Pinkerton bows. Yesterday, says Butterfly, she went to the mission; she is ready to adopt Pinkerton's faith but her family does not know. [Since Pinkerton spent a hundred yen to have her, she promises to be frugal.] She will perhaps even forget her family [and she throws away the ottoke.]

The marriage ceremony begins. The commissioner authorizes the marriage of Pinkerton (by his own will) and Butterfly of Omara, Nagasaki (by consent of her relatives). They sign. Congratulations follow. Sharpless and the officials leave. Pinkerton [offers food and drinks, then] wants to finish the party. The relatives toast the couple. [Butterfly wishes them to leave. Uncle Yakuside sings a comical song.] The bonze arrives and curses Butterfly because of her visit to the mission and her abandonment of the ancient faith. All relatives renounce Butterfly and leave.

Butterfly cries but then overcomes her sadness as Pinkerton comforts her. She kisses his hand as a sign of respect. The maid Suzuki says her evening prayers. It is getting dark. Butterfly feels happy now. She dresses in white for the night, while Pinkerton calls her a squirrel and a plaything, then he says, "my wife." He wants Butterfly to say that she loves him. Butterfly answers that she feels like the moon goddess who knows love but hesitates to name it for fear of dying. "Love doesn't kill," says Pinkerton. [Butterfly recalls that she wanted to marry "for a while" but when Goro recommended Pinkerton she refused initially because she thought Americans were barbarians.] Now Pinkerton has become for her the eye of the firmament. She liked him as soon as she met him. She wants his love even if it's just a small amount, because Japanese are used to tiny things. Pinkerton praises her name but this frightens Butterfly because foreigners pin butterflies. So they cannot fly away, says Pinkerton. Together they watch the night and express their passion. Butterfly tells him that this is for life.

## Act 2

It is three years later and Pinkerton has left Japan. Suzuki is praying before the statue of Buddha. Butterfly expresses some preference for the American god. Money has almost run out but Butterfly trusts Pinkerton, who had promised to return when the robins nest. She tells the doubtful Suzuki that one fine day Pinkerton will come back in his white ship and will climb the hill and join her.

Sharpless arrives with a letter from Pinkerton. He cannot answer Butterfly's question about the robins. Butterfly tells him how Goro (who came with Sharpless) tried to marry her to Prince Yamadori. Then Yamadori also arrives and promises Butterfly faithfulness, but Butterfly answers that she is married and that divorce, while easy in Japan, is difficult in America. Sharpless tells Yamadori that Pinkerton is returning to Nagasaki and asked him to prepare Butterfly for the fact that he does not want to see her again. Yamadori says he is still hoping for Butterfly's favors and leaves with Goro.

Finally, Sharpless can read Pinkerton's letter but he is often interrupted by Butterfly, who does not grasp what is going on. When Sharpless finally asks her what she would do should Pinkerton not return, Butterfly answers that she could become a geisha again or die. When Sharpless uses the occasion to advise her to accept Yamadori's offer, she understands. She disappears and comes back with the boy she had with Pinkerton. In an emotional outburst, she asks Sharpless to tell Pinkerton that he has a son. Passionately, Butterfly tells the child that Sharpless wants her to go back to her old life of dancing and singing but she would rather die. [In the initial version, instead of this language, she has a vision of meeting the emperor and talking to him about her case. The emperor makes her son a prince.] She tells Sharpless that the boy's name is Dolore (Trouble) but when his father returns it will be changed into Gioia (Joy). Sharpless promises to inform Pinkerton and leaves.

Suzuki drags in Goro, who has been gossiping about the boy's allegedly unknown father; Goro leaves. A cannon shot is heard. Butterfly and Suzuki see Pinkerton's ship arrive. Butterfly is triumphant. [She tells the child that now his name is Joy.] The women decorate the house with flowers for Pinkerton's expected arrival. Butterfly dresses in her wedding obi. As the night falls, she makes three holes in the paper screen for them to look outside. The women and the boy wait through the night for Pinkerton's return.

## Act 3

When the sun rises, Suzuki and Dolore have fallen asleep but Butterfly is still waiting. She sings a lullaby for the boy, then withdraws with him for a rest. Pinkerton and Sharpless arrive with an American woman, whom they leave outside when they enter. The men tell Suzuki that she is Kate, Pinkerton's wife, and ask Suzuki to prepare Butterfly for abandoning Dolore to the Pinkertons. Sharpless makes bitter reproaches to Pinkerton about his past behavior. Pinkerton gives him money for Butterfly, expresses his remorse, bids farewell to the little house (the aria "Addio Fiorito Asil" was added after the initial performance in La Scala), and rushes out. Suzuki promises Kate that she will try to help Butterfly. When Butterfly enters, Suzuki tells her that Pinkerton will not come back. Butterfly sees Kate [who explains who she is, tells her that she will take good care of Dolore, and asks for Butterfly's forgiveness]. Sharpless asks Butterfly to make the sacrifice of her child to Pinkerton. Butterfly says she will comply with her husband's wish. [She refuses the money offered by Sharpless.] She promises to give her son to Pinkerton in half an hour. Sharpless and Kate leave.

Butterfly sends Suzuki away. She prepares her suicide with her father's sword and kneels in front of the statue of Buddha. When Suzuki quietly pushes Dolore into the room, Butterfly bids him an emotional farewell, blindfolds him, and disappears behind a screen. She stabs herself, then reappears. Pinkerton and Sharpless rush in the moment Butterfly dies.

# Chronology

| YEAR | GLOVER FAMILY | BUTTERFLY STORY |
|------|---------------|-----------------|
| 1838 | Thomas B. Glover born in Aberdeen (U.K.) | |
| 1840 | Alexander J. Glover born in Aberdeen (U.K.) | |
| 1849 | Otsuki Tsuru born in Osaka and adopted by Awajiya Yasubei and Sato | Sara Jane Long born in Hanover, Penn. (USA) |
| 1850 | Alfred Glover born in Bridge of Don (U.K.) | |
| 1851 | | Irvin Henry Correll born in Northampton, Penn. (USA) |
| 1858 | | Giacomo Puccini born in Lucca |
| 1859 | Thomas B. Glover arrives in Nagasaki | |
| 1861 | | John Luther Long born |
| 1862 | Awajiya Tsuru marries Yamamura and moves to Hogo Takeda | |
| 1863 | Thomas B. Glover builds his Nagasaki residence, Ipponmatsu (Minami Yamate) | |

| YEAR | GLOVER FAMILY | BUTTERFLY STORY |
|------|---------------|-----------------|
| 1864 | Yamamura divorces his wife Tsuru and she returns to Osaka | |
| | Alex Glover arrives in Nagasaki | |
| 1866 | Alex Glover marries Ann Finlay in Nagasaki | |
| 1867 | Alex and Ann Glover return to Scotland accompanied by Thomas B. Glover | |
| 1868 | Thomas B. Glover returns to Nagasaki together with Alfred Glover | |
| 1869 | Awajiya Tsuru meets Thomas B. Glover in Osaka and joins him in Nagasaki | |
| | Alex Glover returns to Nagasaki | |
| 1870 | Kaga Maki's son Shinsaburo born in Nagasaki's Konya-machi (father: unknown, foreign) | Oyama Hisako born in Nagato (Japan) |
| | Thomas B. Glover's company is declared bankrupt | |
| 1871 | | Irvin Correll marries Sara Jane Long |
| 1873 | | Irvin and Jennie Correll arrive in Japan |
| 1874 | Alex Glover moves to Shanghai | |

| YEAR | GLOVER FAMILY | BUTTERFLY STORY |
|------|---------------|-----------------|
| 1875 | Nakano Ei's daughter Waka born in Yokohama (father: James Walters) | |
| 1876 | Awajiya Tsuru's daughter Hana born in Nagasaki (father: presumably Thomas B. Glover) | |
| | Kaga Shinsaburo moves to Awajiya Tsuru's household in Kojimamachi, Nagasaki, and is now called Awajiya Shinsaburo (adopted by Tsuru at a later, unknown date) | |
| | Nomura Motosuke (father of Mrs. Oyama) visits Nagasaki | |
| 1877 | Kaga Maki marries a Japanese man and moves to Minamitaki | |
| | Thomas B. Glover's bankruptcy is canceled | |
| 1878 | Alfred Glover joins Holme, Ringer and Co. in Nagasaki | |
| | Awajiya Tsuru's unnamed son born; dies in Nagasaki | |
| 1880 | (date approx.) Awajiya Tsuru moves from Kojimamachi to Minami Yamate (Ippon-matsu) | |
| 1881 | Awajiya Shinsaburo joins Cobleigh Seminary in Nagasaki | Caroll Long establishes Cobleigh Seminary in Nagasaki (Higashi Yamate) |

| YEAR | GLOVER FAMILY | BUTTERFLY STORY |
|------|---------------|-----------------|
| 1882 | Alex Glover leaves Shanghai for America | |
| 1884 | | Miura Tamaki is born |
| 1885 | Awajiya Shinsaburo moves to Tokyo to join Gakushuin University | Pierre Loti visits Nagasaki |
| 1887 | Thomas B. Glover, Awajiya Tsuru, and Hana move to Tokyo | |
| 1888 | Kaga Maki divorces and returns to Nagasaki | Pierre Loti publishes *Madame Chrysanthème* |
| | Awajiya Shinsaburo graduates in Tokyo and changes his name to Awajiya Tomisaburo (possibly his adoption by Tsuru is also in this year) | |
| | Thomas B. Glover sells Ippon-matsu to Mitsubishi | |
| 1890 | Nakano Waka adopted by Awajiya Tsuru | |
| 1891 | Awajiya Tomisaburo registers at the University of Pennsylvania under the name Thomas Awajiya Glover. He attends for two years | |
| 1892 | | Irvin and Jennie Correll arrive in Nagasaki and live on Higashi Yamate |

| YEAR | GLOVER FAMILY | BUTTERFLY STORY |
|---|---|---|
| 1893 | | Première of André Messager's *Madame Chrysanthème* |
| 1894 | Awajiya Tsuru moves temporarily back to Nagasaki and has her *koseki* corrected and updated<br><br>Awajiya Tomisaburo joins Holme, Ringer and Co. in Nagasaki; he reestablishes his *koseki* in the name of Guraba | |
| 1896 | Thomas B. Glover moves temporarily back to Nagasaki<br><br>Awajiya Hana returns to Nagasaki and is adopted by Guraba Tomisaburo | |
| 1897 | Guraba Hana marries Walter George Bennett and moves to Inshon (Korea) | Irvin and Jennie Correll leave Nagasaki for Philadelphia; contacts are begun between Jennie Correll and her brother John Luther Long |
| 1898 | | John Luther Long publishes *Madame Butterfly* in the *Century Magazine* |
| 1899 | Awajiya Tsuru dies in Tokyo and is buried in Nagasaki | |

| YEAR | GLOVER FAMILY | BUTTERFLY STORY |
|------|---------------|-----------------|
| 1899 | Guraba Tomisaburo marries Awajiya Waka in Nagasaki | |
| 1900 | | Opening of David Belasco's play *Madame Butterfly* in New York |
| | | Puccini sees Belasco's *Madame Butterfly* in London |
| | | Puccini starts working on his opera with Illica and Giacosa as librettists |
| 1904 | Alfred Glover dies on his way to Scotland and is buried in Nagasaki | Première of Puccini's *Madama Butterfly* at La Scala in Milan |
| | | Performance of modified *Madama Butterfly* in Brescia |
| 1906 | Kaga Maki dies in Nagasaki | Performance of the further modified *Madama Butterfly* in Paris |
| | | Giacosa dies |
| 1911 | Thomas B. Glover dies in Tokyo and is buried in Nagasaki; Tsuru is re-buried with him | |
| 1919 | | Illica dies |
| 1924 | | Puccini dies |
| 1926 | | Irvin Correll dies |
| 1927 | | John Luther Long dies |

| YEAR | GLOVER FAMILY | BUTTERFLY STORY |
|------|---------------|-----------------|
| 1931 | Muramatsu Shofu meets Guraba Tomisaburo in Nagasaki | Jennie Correll gives interviews in Japan and China about the origins of the Butterfly story |
| 1933 | | Jennie Correll dies |
| 1935 | | Miura Tamaki gives interviews about the origins of the *Madame Butterfly* story |
| 1938 | Hana Bennett dies in Inshon and is buried there | |
| 1943 | Guraba Waka dies in Nagasaki and is buried there | |
| 1944 | Walter George Bennett dies in England | |
| 1945 | Guraba Tomisaburo ends his life in Nagasaki and is buried there | |
| 1946 | | Miura Tamaki dies in Tokyo |
| 1955 | | Oyama Hisako dies in Yokohama |

# Notes

## Chapter I The Butterfly Saga: O-Taki-San and O-Kiku-San

1. In another version of the story, she had herself voluntarily registered in the licensed quarter in order to be able to "marry" Siebold, which otherwise would not have been possible for her as an ordinary woman during that period. It is not clear how, in that case, she would have met him.

2. The novel runs from 2 July until 18 September; the real dates in the diary are 8 July until 12 August. But, according to his letter of 9 August, Loti had already left Japan on that date.

3. Loti's use of the term "two families" raises a question: which families? Obviously, there was no French family on Loti's side, so there must have been two Japanese families. The novel doesn't mention any families at the registration ceremony but it does specify the presence of two families at the end of the "look-at" meeting: those of the rejected Jasmin and of Chrysanthème; late in the evening they leave in two different directions. Chrysanthème, not being Kangourou's candidate, must have come at her own initiative—perhaps she was tipped by her cousin the rikshaman and arranged for herself the presence of her family, which would be necessary in case of negotiations with Loti. One cannot but admire her sense of initiative. In his unpublished diary, Loti mentions as the two families those of his "fiancée" and his landlord. It is possible, of course, that Loti's landlord belongs to Jasmin's family.

4. Nothing is known about the date of Bigot's watercolor. It shows Chrysanthème with a parasol in a pose that very much resembles the drawing of Rossi in the original edition of Loti's novel.

5.  This stone only mentions facts, unlike another memorial stone erected in 1950 in Nagasaki's Suwa Park, which reads, "Pierre Loti, great French writer, at that time officer of the navy, visited this port and, inspired by these marvellous landscapes and the melancholy of the journey, wrote a love story full of profound and heartbreaking sadness."

6.  Messager was born in 1853 and died in 1929. He was one of the rare disciples of Camille Saint-Saëns (the other famous one being Gabriel Fauré). He was director of the Opéra Comique, the Opéra de Paris, and the Royal Opera, Covent Garden. He also found time to play the organ of the Eglise St. Sulpice in Paris on Sundays.

## Chapter 2  Japonisme

1.  The term "Japonisme" was first used by the French art critic Philippe Burty in 1872.

2.  For the period 1866 to 1906, I've found some thirty painters, about half of them French, who produced one or more paintings of Japanese or Western women dressed in kimono.

3.  The influential political journalist Kuga Katsunan wrote in 1889, "If we tolerate interference, we shall be classed with Turkey and Egypt." Quoted by Kenneth B. Pyle in *The New Generation in Meiji Japan* (Stanford, Calif.: Stanford University Press, 1969), 115.

4.  Judith Gautier's *Le Livre de Jade* was translated into Italian in 1882 by Tulio Massarani and remained in print until 1909; it made a profound impression on Luigi Illica, who largely borrowed from it for his libretto of *Iris*.

5.  Audrey Williamson, *Gilbert and Sullivan Opera* (London: Marion Boyars, 1982), 169–71.

6.  Leslie Baily, *The Gilbert and Sullivan Book* (London: Spring Books, 1966), 270.

7.  This piano score raises a question, because Italian translations of two

of Gilbert's texts are penciled on it. Why should Puccini need these, since an Italian translation by Gustavo Macchi of the vocal score of the entire work had been available since 1899, printed and published by Puccini's own publisher, Ricordi? There are two copies of this work in the Pierpoint Morgan Library in New York and one of them even shows the wear of hard use in theaters all over Italy! My only explanation is that Puccini had acquired the English score before 1899.

8.   Mosco Carner, *Puccini* (London: Duckworth, 1958), 368.

9.   Mosco Carner, "Debussy and Puccini," *Musical Times*, June 1967, 502–5; Louis Laloy, "L'Opéra," in L. Rohozinsky, ed., *Cinquante ans de Musique Française* (Paris: Librairie de France, 1925), 59 ff.

## Chapter 3   The Butterfly Saga: Cho-Cho-San

1.   The school still exists, now called the Nagasaki Wesleyan Junior College, Chinzei Gakkuin. It is located in Isahaya, just outside Nagasaki.

2.   There are several inaccuracies in the text of the *Jiji Shimpo* article. For example, "thirty-four years ago" refers to the time Mrs. Correll told her brother (1897), not to the time of the event or the time she heard about it herself. Also, Dr. Irvin H. Correll was headmaster and teacher at Chinzei Gakkuin (still called Chinzei Gakkan at that time) but the school had been founded by Dr. Carrol S. Long (no relation to Mrs. Correll and John Luther Long) in 1881 under the name of Cobleigh Seminary. I also note that the term "usual shopkeeper" is the translation of *"de-iri shonin,"* normally used for the salesman where one usually goes for shopping or the salesman who regularly comes to the house to offer merchandise for sale.

3.   The *Century Illustrated Monthly Magazine* 55 (new series 33), November 1897–April 1898, 374–92. The story appeared in book form for the first time (with four others of Long's short stories) in 1898, published by the Century Company of New York. A Japanese translation

(the only one I could find) was published in 1981 by the Nagasaki Wesleyan Junior College with an introduction and an essay on models for Madame Butterfly, both written by Dr. Furusaki Hiroshi.

4. For extracts, see Yokoyama Toshio, *Japan in the Victorian Mind* (London: MacMillan, 1987), chapter 5.

5. I cannot see how one could possibly expect Long and his sister to build into the story clear keys that could help detect real persons behind the story. This would not add anything substantial to the Longs' message and instead would reduce its importance by unwarranted sensationalism and, in the process, expose the author (a lawyer!) and his sister to litigation. The fact that, later on, Long and his sister admitted the existence of real persons behind the story does not contradict this because while there clearly was a real case that started it all in the beginning, they did not give hints at the identity of people concerned. In a personal comment in the 1903 edition of the novel, Long indicates that Butterfly is partly real and partly imaginary, thus confirming that he had written fiction on the basis of a real case.

6. The 1935 printed edition of the play mentions Belasco as the author, adding in brackets that the play is founded on Long's story. Apparently Long was not at all involved in writing the play. Copyright information supplied by the 1935 edition of the play mentions The Century Company as the copyright owner of the story, John Luther Long as the owner of the renewed story (the book), and the David Belasco Literary Trust as the owner of the acting version.

7. If it is his invention. The stage directions for the prologue and epilogue of Messager's *Madame Chrysanthème* suggest transformations of the scene that are very close to Belasco's vigil.

## Chapter 4  The Making of an Opera

1. There is no reason to believe that the initial consulate scene was the original act 2 of Illica's draft. In his letter to Ricordi of 16 November 1902, where he announces the cutting out of the consulate act, Pucci-

ni states that the libretto "is not good from the end of Act II onwards" and "Now, however, I am convinced that the opera must be in two acts!!" This language clearly suggests that the consulate scene was the third act. If ever in the correspondence it was called act 2, that could only be because in the early months of the work the later act I was still called the "prologue."

2.  The final agreement, however, was only to be signed in September 1901, according to Puccini's letter of 20 September to Elvira. George R. Marek, *Puccini* (New York: Simon and Schuster, 1951), 212.

3.  Long's abundant borrowing from Loti did not interfere with this. I can see no conflict between Long's approach of his subject and the numerous details taken, both by Long and Illica, from Loti to dress up their stories. Such a conflict is suggested by Arthur Groos in *The Puccini Companion* (New York: Norton and Company, 1994), 178–79. He contends that Long's story contains "intertextual" criticism of Loti's novel. Groos's argument is based on the similarity of the beginnings of both stories (the discussion between the hero and his friend aboard their ship of a "marriage" in Japan) and the differences between their endings: Loti comes back to find Chrysanthème testing the coins he paid her; Pinkerton comes back with the expectation to see exactly the same thing but, instead, finds the ultimate drama. What Groos overlooks here is that the latter events only happen in Belasco's play and that neither Pinkerton's return nor Butterfly's effective suicide are part of Long's story. The other "proof" of Long's "critical response" to Loti is, according to Groos, the date of 17 September (for the order for Loti's departure in his novel and for the arrival of Pinkerton's ship in Long's), which should imply that "the tragedy of *Madame Butterfly* takes up where the comedy of Madame Chrysanthème leaves off." I find this not very conclusive, the more so as Groos considers the date of the battle of the Yalu (17 September 1894), "telescoped somewhat" into Jennie Correll's original story, to be a real one that allows the dating of real events.

4.  "He possessed burning intensity of feeling but no profundity and no

spirituality. On his own admission he had 'more heart than mind,'"
from Mosco Carner, *Puccini* (London: Duckworth and Co., 1958),
229, and "This composer with such a wealth of inspiration never read
a book," from Richard Specht, *Giacomo Puccini* (London: Dent and
Sons, 1933), 171.

5.  Howard Greenfeld, *Puccini* (London: Robert Hale, 1981), 128–29.

6.  Groos, *The Puccini Companion*, 346.

7.  One can, of course, not ignore other influences on the intermezzo, in
particular the obvious inspiration for Puccini of the musical picture
of the passage from night to sunrise in the prologue of the first act of
Mascagni's *Iris*.

8.  As there is no mention later on of a separate "prologue," I take it that
the expression in this letter simply refers to act I.

9.  When Puccini acknowledged on 1 October 1901, that he received
these two acts, he must have been referring to acts 2 and 3 (the act in
Butterfly's house and the consulate act), which at that time were still
called acts 1 and 2, the later act 1 then still being called "prologue."
The first contribution he received the following month from Giacosa
can only be the act 1 we know now because it refers to the love duet at
its end. There is no later use of the expression "prologue" in the correspondence.

10. Examples: an inspection of Pinkerton's newly rented house with
Sharpless (which comes from Loti's inspection with Yves of the
"minute and comical details" of his house in chapter IV); Pinkerton's
"funny" descriptions of the Japanese (Touki-san reminds him of a
"gaily dressed-up old monkey" and the Japanese women are called
"our little dancing dogs"); the "funny" bowing of the family when
they arrive; the drunk Uncle Yakuside; Butterfly's cousin (Loti's
"cousin" about whom there is "no end of jokes"); and Pinkerton's
offering of refreshments to the family (as Loti does in chapter IV,
while Yves looks at it "with a comical grimace"). The list is far from
complete.

11. More examples of Illica's Americanisms: the "Yankee vagabondo," "America forever" (strangely recalling Kangourou's "Buddha forever" in Messager's *Madame Chrysanthème*), the drinks ("whiskey-bourbon" or "milk-punch"), the "mutual" (English in the text) of love praised by Pinkerton, and the tipping of the Japanese officials by Goro "in the American way." From Long, Illica took Butterfly's notion that Americans are barbarians. Some of these have disappeared in the process but a few snippets survived.

12. Quoted by William Weaver, *Puccini: The Man and His Music* (London: Hutchinson, 1978), 54.

13. The final break with Corinna came sometime in 1903 but the pressure put on him by Elvira and Ricordi (not to mention his sisters) started at least as early as the spring of 1902. Negotiations through lawyers went on until the end of 1903, according to a letter from Elvira to Illica of 24 November 1903.

14. This is suggested by Ubaldo Gardini, visiting professor at Geidai, in a presentation made in Tokyo in March 1987. Of course, Mrs. Oyama could not be seen as a woman of an inferior condition but, as a Japanese, she would fall outside the Italian bourgeois society that seemed to be Puccini's social parameter. In a 1998 article, Professor Sawada Toshio, grandson of Oyama Hisako, firmly limits their contacts to exchanges on Japanese music and the presentation by Mrs. Oyama to Puccini of Japanese scores and records acquired, he affirms, with the help of the pianist Kouda Nobuko in Tokyo.

## Chapter 5  Real-Life Models

1. Among recent attempts, one has to count Arthur Groos, "Madame Butterfly: The Story," *Cambridge Opera Journal* 32 (July 1991): 125–88, which, in spite of the fascinating research it is founded on, is totally unconvincing. Groos identifies the U.S. Navy Ensign William B. Franklin as the Pinkerton of John Luther Long's story. I briefly recall

his argument: in her talks of 1931 in Tokyo, Jennie Correll declared that her brother John Luther asked her to mark in his manuscript of Madame Butterfly "anything not true to the life." Groos concludes that Jennie ensured that her brother's narrative described just "thinly disguised" but otherwise real persons and events. He identifies Pinkerton's friend Sayre as Dr. John S. Sayre, a naval surgeon. He then looks for another officer who was young (as Jennie had stated), had "just" come from the Mediterranean (Long's story), and served with Sayre on the same vessel "on their voyage out" to Nagasaki (again Long's story). According to Groos, he should have been in Nagasaki between 1892 and 1894 after his discussion with Sayre aboard the ship and for a period long enough to arrange for his "marriage." Groos finds in the *Naval Register* that William B. Franklin is the only one who fulfills all these conditions.

All this is not so evident. To begin with, there is the obvious fact that the opening scene, taking place between the two friends on the deck of the ship, is taken from Loti's *Madame Chrysanthème*. Secondly, according to the deck logs quoted by Groos, Franklin returned to the United States from the Mediterranean in July 1890 and arrived in Nagasaki only in April 1892, nearly two years later and not "just" after he left the Mediterranean; Franklin then stayed three weeks in Nagasaki. Franklin came back to Nagasaki in June 1892 on a voyage during which his ship towed Sayre's ship; both were in Nagasaki for the following six weeks but on board two different ships; finally, Franklin came for the third time to Nagasaki in December 1892 for one week and was then joined by Sayre on the same vessel, two days before their final departure. So there could never have been a discussion between the two men on the same deck "on the voyage out." Groos additionally mentions that during his second stay in Nagasaki, Franklin reported to his ship's doctor on 4 July with gonorrhea—proof, Groos contends, of an affair. I find this hardly an indication for the kind of heartbreaking drama that Jennie conveyed to her brother.

The main problem with these "proofs" is that they rest entirely on

Jennie's remark that her brother asked her to note "anything not true to the life." The obvious interpretation of this is that John Luther trusted his sister's judgment on things Japanese; Groos's interpretation is that Long's story must have a high degree of authenticity in terms of real events and persons and that, while real identities had to be protected, the story was to stay as close as possible to reality. I wonder what protection he has in mind if even the name of one participant, Dr. Sayre, is explicitly mentioned.

2.  More quotations from Mrs. Correll can be found in Groos's article, mentioned above.

3.  As for Groos's suggestion that Butterfly would have resided above or behind the concession in "Naminohira-yama or South Hill," I observe that Naminohira is an old name for Minami Yamate (South Hill); maps of Nagasaki of that time clearly show that no houses or other buildings existed "above or behind" the concession, the mountain behind Minami Yamate being too steep to construct anything.

4.  This was the case, for example, of the merchant Thomas B. Glover, who had a registered house in Kojimamachi that was used by his common-law wife Awajiya Tsuru and her children.

5.  Miura Tamaki (1884–1946) was Japan's first international soprano, who started an impressive worldwide career in 1914 when she made her debut in London as the leading role in *Madama Butterfly*. In her memoirs, she describes her meetings with Giacomo Puccini and John Luther Long. A memorial has been erected for her in the Kaneiji Dai Ni Reien cemetery, in Tokyo's downtown district Ueno, in the form of a large stone butterfly.

6.  There is some information available about cases of suicide and attempted suicide in Nagasaki, based on research done by Dr. Furusaki Hiroshi, chairman of the board of trustees of Nagasaki Wesleyan Junior College, and reported in a comment in the Japanese edition of Long's novel published by the college in 1981. But his information is, unfortunately, incomplete and inconclusive.

7.  Miura Tamaki's story has been reported by at least four different

authors, i.e., by Michael Teague, Charles Osborne (who told me that Mary Jane Matz was his source), Mosco Carner, and David Alexander Terry. Some of these but not all have linked the story to Long. It seems obvious to me that Miura Tamaki could have heard Tom Glover's name only from the Longs, who were the original source of the whole story and both of whom she met (Jennie in Nagasaki in 1922 and John in Philadelphia around 1925). Miura Tamaki also met Oyama Hisako, whose eldest daughter was her Italian-language teacher (according to her son, Professor Sawada), but there is no proof that Mrs. Oyama knew any of the real names of the concerned persons.

8. Noda Heinosuke was married to a granddaughter of Awajiya Tsuru's daughter Sen. He came several times to Nagasaki to explore the family of his wife's great-grandmother. His book of 1972 is a report on his findings in Nagasaki. In *Mo Hitori no Cho-cho-fujin* (published in 1997 by Mainichi Shimbunsha), Noda Heinosuke's daughter Kazuko states that Tomisaburo was Tsuru's natural child, and that the mention of Kaga Maki as his mother in her *koseki* was faked in order to give the boy the status of a Japanese citizen. Subsequent "adoption" by Tsuru brought Tomisaburo legally back to his natural mother, she says. The *koseki* reproduced in *Mo Hitori no Cho-cho-fujin* (different from those I obtained in Nagasaki) do not reveal whether they are faked or not. The alleged absence of children in Kaga Maki's own *koseki* is not very convincing since the Glover family photo albums refer to them. A photo of Tsuru with a baby reproduced in *Mo Hitori no Cho-cho-fujin* seems to me to show Hana. Also, I wonder what citizenship rights Tomisaburo would have acquired as son of an unmarried, Japanese Maki that he wouldn't have received as son of an unmarried, Japanese Tsuru.

9. The incorporation of Tsuru in the Guraba family was apparently important. Tsuru's original tombstone mentions explicitly that she was the mother of Guraba Tomisaburo (which she was through adoption

only) and omits her own name, Awajiya. The reason might be the need to get rid of the name Awajiya, which is a name belonging to one of the lower classes, whereas Guraba clearly suggests a samurai background.

10. Details of the last years of Guraba Tomisaburo and Waka were conveyed to me by Albert Walker, the last descendant with a British name of the foreign settlers in Nagasaki and during the years of World War II a very young son of Guraba's neighbors. He told me the moving story of how he discovered Tomisaburo's suicide in the middle of the indescribable chaos and misery that reigned in Minami Yamate during the weeks following the explosion of the nuclear bomb in Nagasaki.

11. There is no reference in Jennie Correll's story to a naval officer, and Long flatly denies any link with the U.S. Navy; in his preface to the 1903 edition of *Madame Butterfly* by the Century Company, Long (in his usual, ineffective tongue-in-cheek style) affirms: "And where is Pinkerton? At least not in the Unites States Navy—if the savage letters I receive from his fellows are true." His denial of a link with the navy is confirmed by his statement to Miura Tamaki that the father of Tom Glover had not been a naval officer but an English merchant.

12. Thomas Glover had in December 1861 a son, Umekichi, with a Japanese woman called Sono; the child died in April 1862. He had another son John (mother unknown), born in September 1865, who was registered three months later at the U.K. consulate in Nagasaki; the registration was deleted at a later, unknown date. With Tsuru he had a daughter, Hana, born on 8 August 1876, who married W. G. Bennett in 1897 and who died in 1938 in Inshon, Korea. Finally, he had an unnamed son, born in June 1878 from Tsuru, who died the same year and whose ashes are buried with those of his mother.

13. I found this information in Groos's article. Groos concludes that Mrs. Correll made a mistake and meant to say, "when they first arrived in Nagasaki." But what she said makes perfect sense as it implies a timing that fits the real events: Cho-san lived very near the Corrells' (later)

home on Higashi Yamate at the time they first arrived in Japan in
1873. More circumstantial proof that Long must have known that
the real events were more than twenty years old is supplied by the story itself, where Butterfly tells that she "married" Pinkerton "just" after
her father killed himself; as her father was a samurai who committed
suicide during the Satsuma rebellion of 1877, Long must have been
aware that Butterfly's "marriage" with Pinkerton took place during the
seventies and not the nineties.

14. See *The Diary of Kido Takayoshi*, vol. 3 (Tokyo: University of Tokyo
Press, 1986).

15. Some authors think that the link between Madame Butterfly and the
Glover/Guraba families was just made up after World War II to pro-
mote tourism (see the Preface of this book). I note, however, that
Muramatsu Shofu already knew of its existence when he visited Guraba Tomisaburo in 1931.

## Chapter 6  *Madama Butterfly* in Japan

1. Regarding G .V. Rossi and his efforts to familiarize the Japanese public with Western opera, see Edward Seidensticker, *Low City, High City*
(New York: Knopf, 1983), 268.

2. It is certainly surprising to see Puccini make this mistake, since he was
particularly interested in Buddhism and intended at one time to write
an opera on the life of Buddha.

3. Ivan Morris, *The Nobility of Failure* (New York: Penguin Books, 1975).

4. This judgment refers to the old Japanese family, but I think many
modern Japanese are still conscious of it.

## Afterword

1. Professor Charles Boxer of the United Kingdom kindly conveyed to
me some memories of a visit to Ippon-matsu in the mid-1930s, where
he shared the company of Tomisaburo and "two beautiful Eurasian
girls," Hana's daughters.

2. Richard Storry, *A History of Modern Japan* (New York: Penguin Books, 1984), chapter 8.

3. I have tried to verify this point with Edward Seidensticker, who was with the U.S. occupation forces in Kyushu in 1945. Seidensticker has doubts about Walker's observation because Tomisaburo's suicide occurred on 26 August and the first American troops only disembarked on 1 September. Albert Walker, in his discussions with me, was absolutely positive about the event he witnessed. At that time, Albert was six years old. Could he be, even at that age, mistaken about seeing his first American soldier, who was also the first black man he had ever seen? I am convinced that Albert is right and that either some advanced American units already landed in August to prepare quarters or the recorded date of Tomisaburo's death is wrong and must be corrected toward early September.

# Bibliography

## Chapter I  The Butterfly Saga: O-Taki-San and O-Kiku-San

### ON SIEBOLD AND OTHER FOREIGNERS DURING THE EDO PERIOD

Bowes, John Z. *Western Medical Pioneers in Feudal Japan*. Baltimore: The Johns Hopkins Press, 1970.

Boxer, C. R. *Jan Compagnie in Japan, 1600–1850*. 2d. ed. The Hague: M. Nijhoff, 1950.

Daudet, Alphonse. *Contes de Lundi*. Paris: A. Lemerre Ed., n.d.

Pompe van Meerdervoort, J. L. C. *Doctor on Desima*. Tokyo: Sophia University, 1970.

Smith, George. *Ten Weeks in Japan*. London: Longman, Green, Longman and Roberts, 1861.

### ON MADAME CHRYSANTHÈME, PIERRE LOTI, AND ANDRÉ MESSAGER

Blanch, Leslie. *Pierre Loti*. London: Collins, 1983.

Farrère, Claude. *Loti*. Paris: Flammarion, 1930.

Février, Henri. *André Messager, mon Maître, mon Ami*. Paris: Amiot-Dumond, 1948.

Funaoka, Suetoshi. *Pierre Loti et l'Extrême-Orient*. Tokyo: France Tosho, 1988.

Loti, Pierre. *Madame Chrysanthème*. Paris: Calmann-Lévy, 1888.

―――. *Madame Chrysanthème*. Translated by Laura Ensor. 1888. Reprint, London: K. P. I. Ltd., 1985.

―――. *Madame Chrysanthème suivi de Femmes Japonaises*. Puiseaux: Pardes, 1988.

————. *Japoneries d'Automne*. Paris: Calmann-Lévy, 1889.

————. *La Troisième Jeunesse de Madame Prune*. Paris: Calmann-Lévy, 1905.

————. *Lettres à Madame Juliette Adam (1880–1922)*. Paris: Plon, 1924.

Messager, André. *Madame Chrysanthème: Comédie Lyrique, poème de G. Hartmann et A. Alexandre*. Paris: Choudens, 1893.


## Chapter 2  Japonisme

GENERAL INFORMATION ABOUT JAPONISME

Chamberlain, Basil Hall. *Things Japanese*. London: Kegan Paul, Trench, Trubner, 1891.

Checkland, Olive. *Britain's Encounter with Meiji Japan*. London: MacMillan, 1989.

*Japonisme in Art: An International Symposium*. Society for the Study of Japonisme, Committee for the Year 2001. Tokyo: Kodansha International, 1980.

Matsukata-Reischauer, Haru. *Samurai and Silk*. Cambridge, Mass.: Harvard University Press, 1986.

Okuma, Shigenobu (ed). *Fifty Years of New Japan*. London: Smith, Elder, 1909.

Pyle, Kenneth B. *The New Generation in Meiji Japan*. Stanford: Stanford University Press, 1969.

Storry, Richard. *A History of Modern Japan*. New York: Penguin Books, 1984.

Yokoyama, Toshio. *Japan in the Victorian Mind*. London: MacMillan, 1987.


ON KAWAKAMI SADAYAKKO

Edwards, Osmon. *Japanese Plays and Playfellows*. London: William Heinemann, 1901.

Pantzer, Peter. "Kawakami Otojiro and Sadayakko in Germany, Austria, and Switzerland." Contribution to the International Symposium on the Conservation of Cultural Property, organized by the Tokyo National Research Institute of Cultural Properties, Japan, 1998.

CATALOGUES AND COLLECTIONS

"Le Japonisme." Musée Nationale d'Art Occidental, Tokyo, 1988.

"Toulouse-Lautrec." Musée d'Art Isetan, Tokyo, 1982.

"Vincent van Gogh and Japan." National Museum of Modern Art, Kyoto, 1992.


ON JAPONISME IN MUSIC

Faure, Michel. *Musique et Société du Second Empire*. Paris: Flammarion, Editions Harmoniques, 1985.

Fleury, Michel. *L'Impressionisme et la Musique*. Paris: Fayard, 1996.

Gregor-Dellin, Martin. *Richard Wagner*. Paris: Fayard, 1991.

Larguier, Léo. *Théophile Gautier*. Paris: Tallandier, 1948.

Rohozinsky, L. *Cinquante Ans de Musique Française (1874–1925)*. 2 volumes. Paris: Librairie de France, Editions Musicales, 1925.


LIBRETTOS

Gautier, Judith. *La Marchande de Sourires*. Japanese play in three acts with music by Benedictus. Paris: Charpentier, 1888.

Jones, Sidney. *The Geisha*. On a text by Owen Hall and Harry Greenbank. London: Hopwood and Crew, n.d.

Mascagni, Pietro. *Iris*. Opera di Luigi Illica. Milan: Ricordi, 1898.

————. *Iris*. Opera in three acts on a libretto by Luigi Illica. London: Ricordi, 1907.

Saint-Saëns, Camille. *La Princesse Jaune*. Comic opera in one act on a text of Louis Gallet. Paris: Calmann-Lévy, n.d.


ON GILBERT AND SULLIVAN AND *THE MIKADO*

Allen, Reginald. *Sir Arthur Sullivan*. New York: Pierpoint Morgan Library, 1975.

Baily, Leslie. *The Gilbert and Sullivan Book*. London: Spring Books, 1966.

Williamson, Audrey. *Gilbert and Sullivan Opera*. London: Marion Boyars, 1982.

## Chapter 3  The Butterfly Saga: Cho-Cho-San

ON "MADAME BUTTERFLY" (THE SHORT STORY AND THE THEATER PLAY)

Belasco, David. *Madame Butterfly (A Tragedy of Japan in One Act)*. Based on John Luther Long's story. New York: Samuel French, 1935.

Groos, Arthur. *Madame Butterfly: The Story*. In *Cambridge Opera Journal* 3: 2 (July 1991): 125–58.

Long, John Luther. *Madame Butterfly*. Century Illustrated Magazine 55 (new series 33), November 1897–April 1898.

———. *Madame Butterfly*. New York: Century, 1898, 1903.

———. *Cho-cho-fujin.* Japanese translation. Isahaya: Nagasaki Wesleyan Junior College, 1981.

ON ASPECTS OF JAPANESE LIFE DURING THE MEIJI PERIOD

Cary, Otis. *A History of Christianity in Japan.* Tokyo: Charles E. Tuttle, 1982.

Hearn, Lafcadio. *Japan: An Attempt at Interpretation.* London: MacMillan, 1907.

Mitford, A. B. *The Execution by Hara-Kiri.* Cornhill Magazine 20 (1869) : 549 ff.

Morris, Ivan. *The Nobility of Failure.* New York: Penguin Books, 1975.

Pinguet, M. *Der Freitod in Japan.* Frankfurt: Eichborn, 1996.

Yokoyama, Toshio. *Japan in the Victorian Mind.* London: MacMillan, 1987.

PRESS ARTICLES

*The Japan Times.* 15 March 1931.
*The Japan Magazine.* 21, 1931.
*Jiji Shimpo.* 13 March 1931.

## Chapter 4  The Making of an Opera

On Giacomo Puccini and *Madama Butterfly*

Ashbrook, William. *The Operas of Puccini*. Oxford: Oxford University Press, 1985.

Carner, Mosco. *Puccini*. London: G. Duckworth and Co, Ltd, 1958.

————. *Debussy and Puccini*. In *Musical Times* (London), June 1967: 502–5.

Fiorentino, Dante del. *L'immortel Bohème*. Paris: Robert Laffont, 1953.

Gardini, Ubaldo. "The Betrayal of Madame Butterfly." English translation of an article published by Tokyo Geidai Ongaku Gakubu, March 1987.

Greenfeld, Howard. *Puccini*. London: Robert Hale, 1981.

Groos, Arthur. "Lieutenant F. B. Pinkerton: Problems in the Genesis and Performance of Madama Butterfly." In *The Puccini Companion*, ed. W. Weaver and S. Puccini. New York: Norton, 1994.

Marek, George R. *Puccini*. New York: Simon and Schuster, 1951.

Osborne, Charles. *The Complete Operas of Puccini*. New York: Da Capo Press, 1983.

Sawada, Toshio. *"Chocho Fujin" to Sobo Oyama Hisako*. 113–18, *Chuo Koron*, July 1998, pp. 182–95.

Specht, Richard. *Giacomo Puccini*. London: Dent and Sons, 1933.

Weaver, William. *Puccini: The Man and His Music*. London: Hutchinson, 1978.


Collections of Letters

Adami, Giuseppe. *Letters of Giacomo Puccini*. London: Harrap, 1974.

Gara, Eugenio, ed. *Carteggi pucciniani*. Milan: Ricordi, 1958.


Librettos

*L'avant-scène Opéra No. 56*. Paris: Ed. Premières Loges, 1993.

*Seven Puccini Librettos*. Translated by William Weaver. New York: Norton, 1981.

*Tutti i libretti di Puccini*. A cura di Enrico Maria Ferrando. Milan: Garzanti, 1984.

OPERA PROGRAMS OF *MADAMA BUTTERFLY* PERFORMANCES

*Opera Guide* 26. London: John Calder, 1984.
The Royal Opera, London, 1992.
The Santa Fé Opera, 31st season, 1987.

## Chapter 5  Real-Life Models

MODELS FOR BUTTERFLY, PINKERTON, AND TROUBLE

Furusaki, Hiroshi, ed. *Cho-cho-fujin* [Long's "Madame Butterfly" in Japanese translation]. Isahaya: Nagasaki Wesleyan Junior College, 1981.
Groos, Arthur. *Madame Butterfly: The Story*. In *Cambridge Opera Journal* 3:2 (July): 125–58.
Teague, Michael. "Madame Butterfly: The Real Story." *Opera News* (New York), 3 April 1976.

ON THE GLOVER/GURABA FAMILIES

Earns, Lane R., and Brian Burke-Gaffney. *Across the Gulf of Time (The International Cemeteries of Nagasaki)*. Nagasaki: Nagasaki Bunkensha, 1991.
*Guraba Tei Monogatari*. Collection of local stories published by the city of Nagasaki, 1968.
*Japan Directory*. Lists of foreign residents in China, Japan, and the Philippines, 1864–1912.
Kishimoto, Myoko, ed. *Koe—Ochofujin—Miura Tamaki*. Tokyo: Fubunsha, 1947.
McKay, A. *Scottish Samurai: Thomas Blake Glover, 1838–1911*. Edinburgh: Canongate Press, 1993.
Noda, Heinosuke. *Guraba Fujin*. Nagasaki: Shinnami, 1972.
Williams, Harold S. *The Story of Holme, Ringer and Co., Ltd.* Tokyo: Charles E. Tuttle, 1968.

PRESS ARTICLES

*China Press.* 2 May 1931.
*Japan Magazine.* 21, 1931.
*Japan Times.* 15 March1931.
*Jiji Shimpo.* 13 March 1931, 24 December 1935.
*Nagasaki Shimbun.* Article by Ano Kametoshi. Nagasaki, 15 April 1985.
*New York Times.* 10 November 1933.


## Chapter 6  *Madama Butterfly* in Japan

Finn, Dallas. *Meiji Revisited.* New York: Weatherhill, 1995.
Hearn, Lafcadio. *Japan: An Attempt at Interpretation.* London: MacMillan, 1907.
Morris, Ivan. *The Nobility of Failure.* New York: Penguin Books, 1975.
Okuma, Shigenobu, ed. *Fifty Years of New Japan.* London: Smith, Elder, 1909.
Pinguet, M. *Der Freitod in Japan.* Frankfurt: Eichborn, 1996.
Reed, Edward J. *Japan: Its History, Traditions, and Religions.* 2d. ed. London: Murray, 1880.
Seidensticker, Edward. *Low City, High City: Tokyo, 1867–1923.* New York: Knopf, 1983.
————. *Tokyo Rising: The City Since the Great Earthquake.* New York: Knopf, 1990.


PRESS ARTICLES

Cohen, Aaron M. "Butterfly's Metamorphosis." *Japan Times Weekly,* 14 October 1995.
Fox, Dennis. "Tamaki Miura: The Incomparable Butterfly." *Japan Times,* 14 August 1988.
Seigle, Cecilia Segawa. "A Samurai's Daughter." *Opera News* (New York), 8 January 1994.
Shimazu, Yumiko. "An Unequal Relationship." *Japan Times Weekly,* 14 October 1995.

# Index of Personal Names

STONE BRIDGE PRESS, P.O. BOX 8208, BERKELEY, CA 94707

To comment on this book or to receive a free catalogue of other books about Japan and Japanese culture, contact Stone Bridge Press at sbp@stonebridge.com or 1-800-947-7271.